"How do we think about someone who is not merely 'out there' but also in, with, and through us? Fred Sanders has set out to do just such thinking. The result is a study on the Holy Spirit that comes like a breath of fresh air where familiar terms and images take on new and unexpected significances."

Simon Chan, Former Professor of Systematic Theology, Trinity Theological College, Singapore; Editor, *Asia Journal of Theology*

"*The Holy Spirit: An Introduction* comes with all the hallmarks we anticipate enjoying in a book by Fred Sanders: Trinitarian foundations without obfuscation; appreciation of rigorous theology without ignoring biblically informed experience; reading from the ancient fathers that does not bypass more recent Americans, Dutch, French—and even Scottish—authors; a willingness to correct error without developing a harsh spirit; a desire to seek rapprochement where possible without compromising important convictions; and reverence for great theologians without losing an engaging playfulness. This is an introduction in the root sense of the word. Here we are led into the living reality of the 'three person'd God' who makes himself known through the Holy Spirit. There is theological treasure here, beautifully coupled with theological pleasure! What could be better?"

Sinclair B. Ferguson, Chancellor's Professor of Systematic Theology, Reformed Theological Seminary; Teaching Fellow, Ligonier Ministries

"There are many good books on the Holy Spirit, but Fred Sanders has made a most welcome addition to the literature with an approach that is both fresh and faithful. Introducing the theology of the Holy Spirit as part of Trinitarian theology, he shows how the doctrine of the Trinity shapes and informs our understanding of the Holy Spirit. The result is superbly rich, precise, and wonder-inducing, yet at the same time eminently clear and accessible."

Michael Reeves, President and Professor of Theology, Union School of Theology

"Fred Sanders's little treasure on the Holy Spirit is both theologically rich and spiritually bracing in short compass. You will find yourself invoking, praising, and knowing the blessed Holy Spirit better to your soul's benefit."

Liam Goligher, Senior Minister, Tenth Presbyterian Church, Philadelphia, Pennsylvania

"In his customarily clear, creative, and compelling way, Fred Sanders invites us to consider the Holy Spirit, first, as the divine Trinitarian person whom we already know, and, second, as the subject of theological study. This book covers all its essential aspects, with several unique emphases: an appeal to pneumatology as the doctrine that connects all other doctrines; the proposal that we encounter the Spirit as 'the Holy Presupposition' and appropriate him as the consummating person; the question of what alternatives we have created as substitutes for the Spirit; and twenty-seven 'rules for thinking well about the Holy Spirit.' Vintage Sanders and, thus, a must-read!"

Gregg R. Allison, Professor of Christian Theology, The Southern Baptist Theological Seminary; Secretary, Evangelical Theological Society; author, *God, Gift, and Guide: Knowing the Holy Spirit*

"Fred Sanders is a world-class theologian of the Trinity. In this book, he introduces us to the Holy Spirit—the member of the Godhead whom Christians already know yet often neglect or misunderstand. Accessibly written, rich in historical and theological insight, and unwaveringly faithful to Scripture and orthodoxy, *The Holy Spirit: An Introduction* is the best book of its kind. It distills a great depth of learning into a clear, friendly, pastoral text. The twenty-seven rules of the appendix alone would make a wonderful primer for every Christian."

Gavin Ortlund, author, *Theological Retrieval for Evangelicals*

The Holy Spirit

SHORT STUDIES IN SYSTEMATIC THEOLOGY

Edited by Graham A. Cole and Oren R. Martin

The Atonement: An Introduction, Jeremy Treat (2023)

The Attributes of God: An Introduction, Gerald Bray (2021)

The Church: An Introduction, Gregg R. Allison (2021)

The Doctrine of Scripture: An Introduction, Mark D. Thompson (2022)

Faithful Theology: An Introduction, Graham A. Cole (2020)

Glorification: An Introduction, Graham A. Cole (2022)

The Holy Spirit: An Introduction, Fred Sanders (2023)

Justification: An Introduction, Thomas R. Schreiner (2023)

The Person of Christ: An Introduction, Stephen J. Wellum (2021)

The Trinity: An Introduction, Scott R. Swain (2020)

The Holy Spirit

An Introduction

Fred Sanders

CROSSWAY®

WHEATON, ILLINOIS

Library of Congress Cataloging-in-Publication Data

Names: Sanders, Fred (Fred R.), author.
Title: The Holy Spirit : an introduction / Fred Sanders.
Description: Wheaton, Illinois : Crossway, 2023. | Series: Short studies in systematic theology | Includes bibliographical references and index.
Identifiers: LCCN 2022058979 (print) | LCCN 2022058980 (ebook) | ISBN 9781433561436 (trade paperback) | ISBN 9781433561437 (epub) | ISBN 9781433561443 (pdf)
Subjects: LCSH: Holy Spirit—Biblical teaching.
Classification: LCC BT121.3 .S37 2023 (print) | LCC BT121.3 (ebook) | DDC 231/.3—dc23/eng/20230503
LC record available at https://lccn.loc.gov/2022058979
LC ebook record available at https://lccn.loc.gov/2022058980

To Biola University, with gratitude for
a place to teach and learn

And Torrey Honors College, for a place to talk and read

And Grace Evangelical Free Church,
for a place to pray and serve

Contents

Series Preface

The ancient Greek thinker Heraclitus reputedly said that the thinker has to listen to the essence of things. A series of theological studies dealing with the traditional topics that make up systematic theology needs to do just that. Accordingly, in each of these studies, a theologian addresses the essence of a doctrine. This series thus aims to present short studies in theology that are attuned to both the Christian tradition and contemporary theology in order to equip the church to faithfully understand, love, teach, and apply what God has revealed in Scripture about a variety of topics. What may be lost in comprehensiveness can be gained through what John Calvin, in the dedicatory epistle of his commentary on Romans, called "lucid brevity."

Of course, a thorough study of any doctrine will be longer rather than shorter, as there are two millennia of confession, discussion, and debate with which to interact. As a result, a short study needs to be more selective but deftly so. Thankfully, the contributors to this series have the ability to be brief yet accurate. The key aim is that the simpler is not to morph into the simplistic. The test is whether the topic of a short study, when further studied in depth, requires some unlearning to take place. The simple can be amplified. The simplistic needs to be corrected. As editors, we believe that the volumes in this series pass that test.

While the specific focus varies, each volume (1) introduces the doctrine, (2) sets it in context, (3) develops it from Scripture, (4) draws the various threads together, and (5) brings it to bear on the Christian life. It is our prayer, then, that this series will assist the church to delight in her triune God by thinking his thoughts—which he has graciously revealed in his written word, which testifies to his living Word, Jesus Christ—after him in the powerful working of his Spirit.

Graham A. Cole and Oren R. Martin

Introduction

Haunted by the Holy Ghost

This book introduces Christians to the Holy Spirit, which is a cheeky thing to do.

By definition, every Christian must already know the Holy Spirit in the most important way, since "anyone who does not have the Spirit of Christ does not belong to him" (Rom. 8:9). So to publish a book for Christian readers under the title *The Holy Spirit: An Introduction* is to take on a peculiar project: introducing readers to somebody they already know. That is exactly what this book does. It presupposes that its readers are already engaged with the reality of the Holy Spirit and invites them to a theological encounter with that person.

The Holy Spirit in Three Points

Normally when we grow in our knowledge of people, we say that while we knew them already, now we know them better. But in the case of the Holy Spirit, something more subtle and paradoxical takes place. The Holy Spirit is more than just the next person to know. To encounter him is to be caught up into an act of knowing that claims us altogether and sets us free, that expands our theological horizons while regathering our mental powers, that suspends us in his power and grounds us in his truth. You can't just walk up to him and say hi. Meeting the Holy Spirit, in whom we live and move and have our being, requires a special approach because knowledge of the Spirit is a special kind of knowledge.

We will approach the doctrine of the Holy Spirit obliquely because of who he is and how he acts. The Holy Spirit points in three different directions: he points to the Son, he points back to us, and he points to all truth.

1. *The Holy Spirit points to the Son.* He is deflective, turning our gaze away. There is something slippery about this, because even when the Holy Spirit opens our eyes to see and understand his work, what he primarily directs our attention to is not himself but Jesus Christ. Think of the steps by which our knowledge of the Spirit advances. We start with Jesus. As we understand Jesus Christ more fully, we recognize him not in an isolated way but as the one sent by God the Father. You cannot know one without the other. When Jesus is in the foreground, God the Father is, so to speak, in the background as the one who so loved the world that he gave his only-begotten Son. And then, finally, as we become more aware of this Father-Son relation, we become aware that our awareness of it is being brought about by the Holy Spirit. So when the Holy Spirit, the life-giving Lord of all, effectively accomplishes his work on our hearts and in our minds, he unveils the fact that he has already been at work in us as he has been successfully directing our attention to Jesus.

The Spirit is expert at deflecting attention away from himself and toward the Son. He tends to deflect attention best at exactly the moment when he is most powerfully present in us! As Pentecostal and charismatic Christians have often pointed out, the people who talk the most about the Holy Spirit are not necessarily the people most influenced by the Holy Spirit. On the contrary, the people most influenced by the Holy Spirit are usually the ones with the most to say about Jesus Christ. This is because the Spirit is powerful and effective at deflecting our attention to the Son rather than drawing it to himself.

2. *The Holy Spirit points to our own spiritual knowledge.* He is reflexive, turning our gaze back to itself. While the Holy Spirit is always at work everywhere, his special ministry involves opening our spiritual eyes to the fact that he is already at work everywhere. God gives us the gift of salvation, which includes the Holy Spirit. But he also gives us that same Holy Spirit precisely to open our eyes to the gift itself: "We have received . . . the Spirit who is from God, that we might understand the things freely given us by God" (1 Cor. 2:12). That is, the Spirit within us is a kind of God-given power of reception by which we understand what God has already given. This work of the Spirit is reflexive, because thinking about the Spirit turns our eyes back upon their own act of seeing, so to speak.

There is something inherently eye opening in all the work of the Holy Spirit. Think of the Trinity's revelation. If the Father is the speaker and the Son is his Word, the Spirit is the one who personally causes our understanding of that Word. So to begin thinking about the Spirit is to begin thinking about thinking, or about the one in whom you've already been doing your thinking, meeting somebody you already know. As Hermann Witsius (1636–1708) said of the Spirit, "He cannot be seen, but in his own light; he cannot be known or acknowledged, but by his own kind and gracious agency."[1] Knowledge of the Spirit is spiritual, and the only way into it is by the Spirit.

---

1. Hermann Witsius, *Sacred Dissertations on the Apostles' Creed* (1823; repr., Grand Rapids, MI: Reformation Heritage, 2010), 2:303.

Of course there's more to the Holy Spirit's work than just enlightening our minds; he produces life and imparts power, and (as we will see in chapter 5), does a whole list of other things that are not merely cognitive or mental. The Holy Spirit is not just in your mind! He brings with him a reality that is more than thoughts and ideas. But his great illuminating work on the Christian mind is what gives the study of the Holy Spirit its paradoxical character. Thinking about the Holy Spirit is like faith looking at its own eyeballs. Talking about the Holy Spirit is like faith saying why it's saying what it's saying while it's still saying it. When you try to focus on pneumatology, you realize that there are at least two meanings to the word *vision* in the ancient Irish hymn "Be Thou My Vision." When you sing it, you are asking, with the saints of all the ages, for God to be the object on which your mental eye focuses (what you see; the vision before you), and also to be the power by which the mental eye can focus on such an object (how you see it; your vision). You are asking God to be simultaneously the vision you see and the vision by which you see. "For with you is the fountain of life; in your light do we see light" (Ps. 36:9).

3. *The Holy Spirit points to all truth*. He is connective. These first two reasons why it is paradoxically powerful to give sustained attention to the Holy Spirit already suggest the third reason: the Spirit uniquely connects all truths to each other. When the Holy Spirit illumines a mind, his work is not so much to bring in a few new ideas (though he can and does do this), but to connect all true ideas about God and salvation in a meaningful way. The Spirit uniquely binds every Christian doctrine to every other Christian doctrine, weaving together the spiritual truth of our faith in an integral way. To think specifically about the Holy Spirit, you have to reach into the very heart of Christian life and doctrine and pull out something

that is linked to everything else, something that is always theologically functioning whenever anything at all is theologically functional. And as you drag it out into the light and begin to analyze it by itself, it starts to look strangely isolated and disconnected. That's because in the very act of dragging it out and analyzing it, you have in fact isolated it and disconnected the most connected thing. If we call this third reason the connective aspect of the Spirit's work, it is because of how enmeshed Spirit-knowledge is in all theological knowledge. It is paradoxical to focus our attention on the work of the Spirit in particular, and in isolation, because the work of the Spirit is characteristically connective, consummating, holistic, and synthetic.

Even when we focus directly on the Holy Spirit as the object or content of our study, he is always more. He is its motivating force, its context, its presupposition, its condition, its meaningful form, its inner power, its atmosphere, its element, its idiom, its orientation, its governor, its medium, its carrier. He is all this for any doctrine we study: divine attributes, creation, providence, salvation, church, and the rest. In studying any of these, as we focus our attention on a specific theological topic, it is only in and with and by the Holy Spirit that we reach true understanding of each spiritual topic. And then when the time comes to study the doctrine of the Holy Spirit, we are at work on something special, because in this doctrine, someone special is uniquely at work within us for knowledge of himself. That someone is at work within us as we think and write and read about him. He is the teacher of the lesson that is himself.

Think of it this way. A pulmonologist, in writing about the functioning of the respiratory tract, obviously doesn't need to disconnect and dissect actual lungs. There is no need to tear them out of the chest! But pulmonology is an extremely apt analogy for pneumatology; to think accurately and meaningfully about the lungs as functioning organs in your chest requires thinking about the entire respiratory system. The subspecialties of pulmonology work their way out from the lungs to consider the circulatory system so that the quality of the blood and its movement from the heart are directly implicated. Not only are the body's other systems and behaviors drawn into the relevant analysis but so is the quality of the environment around the body, most notably the ambient air as it makes its way into the breather. This is the kind of doctrine pneumatology is; it involves the lungs of theology and therefore also the heart and blood and breath of theology. It is here in this doctrine that we ought to recognize the divine environment in which all true theology takes place.

It is tempting to say that this connective aspect of the doctrine of the Holy Spirit makes it an especially difficult area of theology. Perhaps it does. But it is also true that pneumatology is the doctrinal location where we are invited to recognize the spiritual character of all doctrines, of theology itself. It is especially here that we are summoned to see that studying theology is a holy task. The great Methodist theologian William Burt Pope (1822–1903) declared of theology that "every branch of this science is sacred. It is a temple which is filled with the presence of God. From its hidden sanctuary, into which no high priest taken from among men can enter, issues a light which leaves no part dark save where it is dark with excess of glory. Therefore all fit students are worshippers as well as students."[2] All theology should be done in the Spirit; what wakes us up to this is the recognition that the theology of the Holy Spirit should be done in the Spirit.[3] Theology itself is, as it were, haunted by the Holy Ghost.

2. William Burt Pope, *A Compendium of Christian Theology* (London: Wesleyan Conference Office, 1879), 1:5.
3. Andrew Murray remarked, at the beginning of a book on the Spirit, that a real understanding of the Spirit's indwelling presence "would transform all our theology into that

How to Meet the Holy Spirit

This book is an introduction to the Holy Spirit for people who already know the Holy Spirit. Our goal is to make the doctrine about the Holy Spirit clearer, but one way this book will do that is by showing readers just how much they already know about the Holy Spirit. The goal, educationally, is not to write the doctrine of the Spirit on the blank slate of faithless minds but to evoke and draw forth the truth of the Spirit from believers. In order to accomplish this, the book takes an indirect route: it situates the doctrine of the Spirit within the doctrine of the Trinity.

Other books on the Holy Spirit take a more direct approach, and I heartily recommend those books as well (see the Further Reading section). I especially recommend two classic approaches to pneumatology that organize the material in different ways, one according to biblical theology and one according to Christian experience. For the biblical theology approach, Sinclair Ferguson's *The Holy Spirit* is exemplary.[4] Beginning with "the Holy Spirit and His Story," it moves through creation, the incarnation, and Pentecost to the Spirit's work in salvation, church, and eschatology. The alternative approach, starting from Christian experience, is James Buchanan's (1804–1870) book *The Office and Work of the Holy Spirit*,[5] which considers the work of the Spirit "in the conversion of sinners" and then traces "the Spirit's work in the edification of his people after their conversion." Both of these approaches are widespread in the literature of pneumatology because both are excellent methods of arranging the subject. Both are classic in their own ways.

---

knowledge of God which is eternal life." See his *Spirit of Christ: Thoughts on the Indwelling of the Holy Spirit in the Believer and the Church* (London: James Nisbet, 1888), 10.

4. Sinclair B. Ferguson, *The Holy Spirit*, Contours of Christian Theology (Downers Grove, IL: InterVarsity Press, 1996).

5. James Buchanan, *The Office and Work of the Holy Spirit* (Edinburgh: John Johnstone, 1842).

But my approach in this book is, as I said above, indirect, which is why I began by highlighting the paradoxical character of studying the Holy Spirit. I hope to treat the paradoxical character of pneumatology not as a hindrance to be lamented but as a help to be cherished. If knowledge of the Holy Spirit is, in the ways described above, deflective, reflexive, and connective, then an introduction to the Holy Spirit might deliver a great deal of insight by arranging itself in a corresponding way. Think of the implications that follow from the work of the Spirit being deflective, reflexive, and connective. *Deflective* means that when you try to think about the Spirit, you find the Spirit himself changing the subject to the Father and the Son. *Reflexive* means that when you try to think about the Spirit, you find the Spirit himself requiring you to think about yourself and about thinking. *Connective* means that when you try to think about the Spirit, the Spirit himself draws you out into the full scope of all theology. But these things are all beneficial! To study the Holy Spirit according to his own characteristic way of working means to be personally engaged in a total Trinitarian encounter with the truth of God.

We will engage the deflective character of pneumatology not by resisting the Spirit's deflective force but by obeying it and focusing our attention on Jesus Christ and God the Father, as the Spirit himself directs us to. We will engage the reflexive character of pneumatology by considering carefully how the Spirit made himself known to us in the history of revelation and how he is manifest now. And we will make the most of the connective aspect of pneumatology by setting pneumatology deliberately in the context of the most comprehensive and all-encompassing of Christian doctrines, the doctrine of the Trinity.

The plan of approach followed in this book may strike some readers as backward. Instead of building up pneumatology piece by piece, precept on precept, it begins with the big picture and only then moves back to show where some of the parts fit. That apparent backwardness, which is actually thinking from the whole to the parts, is the consequence of this book being a short study in systematic theology rather than in biblical theology. The special contribution of systematic theology to the Christian mind is precisely the ability to handle the large, integrating doctrines of the faith in this way. But even among the many possibilities within systematic theology, one could follow a more inductive approach, rehearsing the basic data and then assembling it into the larger structures. What I want to say is that such books exist, and I encourage you to read them. But it seems to me that a lot of Christians have already heard the doctrine of the Spirit put together in that way. Our goal here is not to overwrite that previous teaching (half-remembered though it may be) or to start over from scratch, but to set in place the comprehensive structures of truth within which you can organize all the Spirit information you probably already have in your mind.

That is the strategy by which this book introduces the Holy Spirit to readers who have already met the Spirit. The goal is to enable us to learn pneumatology by leveraging what we already know about God and the Christian life and becoming alert to the Spirit's presence and power in all of it. The book's outline follows directly from the strategy. After a chapter alerting us to the presence of the Spirit (chapter 1) comes a chapter on the Holy Spirit within the Trinity (chapter 2), followed by one chapter each on the three persons: the Spirit and the Father (chapter 3), the Spirit and the Son (chapter 4), and the Spirit himself (chapter 5).

1

Meeting the Holy Spirit

The Holy Spirit is always already. When you become aware of the presence of the Holy Spirit, you become aware that he was present before you became aware. More than that, the spiritual awareness into which you wake up is itself, you come to learn, wrought by the powerful presence of the Holy Spirit. The Holy Spirit always goes before you and prepares you to meet him when you arrive where he is. He is, to use a theological term, the *prevenient* person in our experience of the Trinity—he goes before. We are always playing catch-up. This is the kind of theological truth that takes time to receive. So let us begin (though the Spirit has already begun!) with a brief meditation on the Holy Spirit's prevenience by way of reflecting on our experience of breath.

Breathe in. Breathe out.

You are borrowing the materials of your own life from the environment in which you exist. The ambient air that rushes into your lungs through your nose and mouth is absolutely necessary to sustain you. A human is a breathing thing. In fact, a complete account of who and what you are would have to acknowledge the air in your environment as a necessary part of what it takes for you to keep being you. It's even tempting to think of the whole system of air around you as part of you. Certainly the air inside your lungs, and the oxygen in your blood, seems to be part of you; there's always some air in you, even though it's constantly being exchanged for new air. From another point of view, though, the airy environment surrounding you is not so much a part of you as you are part of it. Systemically speaking, you are part of a larger complex that includes not only you and all that air, but also whatever else it takes to make that air useful for sustaining you (its mixture of elements, its density and temperature, the amount of pressure it is under, and so on). That's creaturely life. All living creatures are embedded in networks of interdependences rather than existing as sovereign, separate, sealed-off, individual entities. Breathing is "a drawing in of the air; and we are so constructed that something foreign to the constitution of the body is inhaled and exhaled."[1] We all borrow our life from our environments.

God's Breath and Ours

There are two theological applications we can draw from this brief meditation on air, and both have to do with the Holy Spirit and his prevenience. First, it's easy and even natural for us to think of the analogy between our dependence on air and our dependence on God. Both are invisible, both surround us, and both sustain our life. The analogy is limited by the fact that air is just as much a creature as we are, of course.[2] But that's how

1. Gregory of Nyssa, from his "Great Catechetical Oration," translated as "An Address on Religious Instruction," in *Christology of the Later Fathers*, ed. Edward R. Hardy, in collaboration with Cyril C. Richardson (Louisville, KY: Westminster Press, 1954), 273.
2. Richard Baxter (1615–1691) notes that "the dependence of the creature on God, is not to be fully manifest by the dependence of any creature upon another," in his

analogies work; our dependence on the created element of air is not the same thing as, but is in certain specific ways something like, our dependence on the Creator. In both God and the air "we live and move and have our being" (Acts 17:28), but in obviously different ways. When you opened this book about the Holy Spirit and read this chapter inviting you to breathe in and breathe out, you probably immediately sensed the power of the obvious metaphor. Breathing in and out is like prayer, or like practicing the presence of God the Holy Spirit. Again, the Holy Spirit is not air; he surrounds us not atmospherically but in a way that is holy and spiritual. He is always already surrounding us. The Spirit's presence to all creatures—invisible, immediate, intimate—is a vital topic. The Holy Spirit's presence to followers of Jesus is even more personal and profound. The Holy Spirit is (like) the air we breathe.

But the second application of our meditation on air is, I think, less obvious. It may require you to turn your thought patterns inside out for a moment, but it is worth doing. Here it is: though all living creatures exist in some sustaining environment, God does not. God is certainly living but is certainly no creature. Gregory of Nyssa puts it this way:

> We must not imagine that, in the way of our own breath, something alien and extraneous to God flows into him and becomes the divine Spirit in him. . . . For we should degrade the majesty of God's power were we to conceive of his Spirit in the same way as ours. On the contrary, we think of it as a power really existing by itself and in its own special subsistence. It is not able to be separated from God in whom it exists, or from God's Word which it accompanies.[3]

book-length sermon *The Crucifying of the World by the Cross of Christ* (London: Nevill Simmons, 1658), 15–17.

3. Gregory of Nyssa, "Great Catechetical Oration," 273.

The God in whom we live and move and have our being does not live and move and have his being in anything or anyone but himself. There are two ways to say this one thing. Negatively, you could deny that God has any environment around him. Positively, and more substantially, you could assert that God is his own environment. Just as God speaks his holy word, he breathes his holy breath. But unlike human breath, divine breath does not come into God from a surrounding environment and then return to it. God's breath is God. God's Spirit is God. God's environment and conditions of existence are all simply God. Edward Polhill (1622–1694) made the point this way:

> God all-sufficient must needs be his own happiness; he hath his being from himself, and his happiness is no other than his being radiant with all excellencies, and by intellectual and amatorious reflexions, turning back into the fruition of itself. . . . He needed not the pleasure of a world, who hath an eternal Son in his bosom to joy in, nor the breath of angels or men who hath an eternal Spirit of his own.[4]

God has no need of the breath of creatures because he has his own breath within the dynamics of the eternal divine life. Not only that, but God has no need of a region in which to be God or a medium through which to be God. God is omnisufficient, absolutely enough in every way. So this second application of our meditation on air is a contrast; God isn't like creatures. Our breath marks us as necessarily surrounded by something besides ourselves, but God's breath is God. In thinking about the Holy Spirit, we are trying to conceive of the divine life as a life that is always already fully resourced—oxygenated, as it were—from its own inherent resources.

---

4. Edward Polhill, "A View of Some Divine Truths," in *The Works of Edward Polhill* (1678; repr., Morgan, PA: Soli Deo Gloria, 1998), 1.

These two applications of our meditation on air point in two different directions. The first application is about our relationship to God (we need God like air); the second is about God's own inner life (God needs no air). "For my thoughts are not your thoughts, neither are your ways my ways," God says (Isa. 55:8). Likewise, the breath of God is not as the breath of creatures. Creaturely breath marks the point at which creatures draw on resources outside themselves to sustain them. Divine breath marks the opposite: God having life in himself, of himself, from himself, as himself. It's hard to imagine, really, because if we start from our own experience of breath and try to apply it to God, we can only get so far. If I try to picture myself having no need of the air in my environment, I might picture myself in scuba gear or a space suit. Obviously, such technological equipment only proves the point that I need air so badly that in an inhospitable and airless setting, I will avail myself of a wearable, artificial micro-environment to meet my needs. But God has no needs.

We have come to a sort of impasse. In us, breath is the sign of our neediness, but in God it is the sign of his needing nothing. Since *breath* means practically opposite things in the cases of ourselves and God, we might decide that it is unwise or unhelpful to use the same word in both cases. But God is the one who picked out this word as somehow appropriate; God told us in Scripture that he has breath (Gen. 2:7; Pss. 33:6; 104:29).[5] In making this comparison, God summons us to lift our thoughts up higher, starting from what we know in our own experience as breathing creatures and ascending mentally to thoughts worthy of God. Once we recognize these ways in

5. Richard E. Averbeck, "Breath, Wind, Spirit, and the Holy Spirit in the Old Testament," in *Presence, Power and Promise: The Role of the Spirit of God in the Old Testament*, ed. David G. Firth and Paul D. Wegner (Nottingham, UK: Apollos, 2011), 23–37. A short version of this work is available at https://bible.org/.

which God's breath is greater than and different from ours, we also recognize that our mental journey upward was only possible because God created all things with this kind of revelation in mind. God doesn't tell us he breathes just because we happen to be creatures who breathe. No; when he made creatures who breathe, he was making images of his own infinite life, and that life is life in the Spirit. Geerhardus Vos (1862–1949) taught that when we hear God speak of human breath and divine Spirit,

> we have to do here not with a mere human figure used by God in Scripture to indicate relationships within His being. The reverse is true. Breath as a sign of life in living beings is an image in what is created of the particular way in which the Holy Spirit, who is the supervisor of life, receives His personal existence from the Father and Son.[6]

What Vos is getting at is that the living God is the one who truly has breath. His uncreated breath is the archetype, while our creaturely breath is the created, limited, imperfect image of that great original. So even though God is the one who has told us, in Scripture, that he is a living God who breathes spiritually, he did not tell us this so that we would assume he is needy like us. On the contrary, God tells us about his Spirit to help us conceive of his awesome otherness and perfection. God is his own breath and environment and life.

So the analogy, with its points of similarity and difference, is this: our breath is in us, and God's breath is in God. But the purpose of salvation is for God's breath to be in us. When we considered the life of breathing creatures, we were describing physical, biological life. The essence of spiritual life, on the other hand, is life in, or from, the Spirit of God. As Jesus taught

---

6. Geerhardus Vos, *Reformed Dogmatics*, trans. and ed. Richard B. Gaffin Jr. (Bellingham, WA: Lexham Press, 2014), 1:68.

Nicodemus, "that which is born of the flesh is flesh, and that which is born of the Spirit is spirit. Do not marvel that I said to you, 'You must be born again'" (John 3:6–7). By its overuse in Christian talk, the word *spiritual* may fail to turn our minds to the breath of God and our participation in it by grace, but that is the real source of spiritual life and salvation.

Nothing is more fundamental to salvation than God's Spirit becoming the principle of new life in us. But before God's Spirit becomes the principle of new life in believers, the Spirit simply is the principle of God's own life. Before the Spirit is in us, the Spirit is in God. This follows as a natural conclusion of confessing the deity of the Spirit, but once we recognize it, we become deeply conscious that the Holy Spirit is who he is for himself before he does what he does for us. This is perhaps the deepest sense in which the Holy Spirit is always already. Not only is he all around us as our spiritual environment and within us as the principle of new life, but he is infinitely far above us in the depths of God's being. He would always be in God, whether he were ever in us or not. He is, to the depths of divine reality, the prevenient person.

The Holy Presupposition

The Holy Spirit's absolute, perfect prevenience is reflected in his presence to us. It seems to be God's design to deal with us through his Holy Spirit, even though he brings us to a definite awareness of that fact only at a later stage. This is especially clear when we contrast our knowledge of the Holy Spirit with our knowledge of the other two persons of the Trinity, God the Father and God the Son. God's method of bringing believers to conscious awareness of himself seems to be a two-stage process. The first stage is to focus our attention on the Father sending the Son to save us; the second stage is to recognize that the only reason our attention was focused in that way was the presence, power, and person of the Holy Spirit influencing us anonymously in the first phase. We hear the message of the Father and the Son, and then we notice that our hearing of it means we are already in the power of the Spirit.

The same dynamic is at work in Christian prayer. The Holy Spirit primarily moves us to pray to the Father in the name of the Son, and it is generally only in a second moment of awareness that we begin to notice the Spirit at work. In *Mere Christianity*, C. S. Lewis described the structure of Christian prayer using the image of moving down a road:

> An ordinary simple Christian kneels down to say his prayers. He is trying to get into touch with God. But if he is a Christian he knows that what is prompting him to pray is also God: God, so to speak, inside him. But he also knows that all his real knowledge of God comes through Christ, the Man who was God—that Christ is standing beside him, helping him to pray, praying for him. You see what is happening. God is the thing to which he is praying—the goal he is trying to reach. God is also the thing inside him which is pushing him on—the motive power. God is also the road or bridge along which he is being pushed to that goal. So that the whole threefold life of the three-personal Being is actually going on in that ordinary little bedroom where an ordinary man is saying his prayers.[7]

God is the goal and the pathway there, but also the mobilizing energy or "motive power" by which we follow that path to that goal. The characteristic act of Christian faith is to seek God in Christ, to move toward the Father as the goal, and to do so by way of the Son as the road or bridge. The Holy Spirit

7. C. S. Lewis, *Mere Christianity* (New York: Macmillan, 1943), 142–43.

is more or less concealed within that seeking and moving, a personal presence who only dawns on our awareness when we become more self-conscious about what has been happening to us, and by whose power. We say, "God so loved the world, that he gave his only Son" (John 3:16), and then we learn that we know this in the Spirit (John 3:8).

We need a greater authority than C. S. Lewis to demonstrate this, so we should look carefully at some strong scriptural indications of the method God follows. As we turn directly to those passages, I want to emphasize that this divine method is intentional. This is the order in which God intends for us to come to knowledge of Father, Son, and Holy Spirit. The Spirit is a presupposition but not an afterthought. We are affected by him first but learn of him last. And this is not some sort of divine sloppiness (as if there were such a thing). This is how it is supposed to work; this is how God intends to be known. Experiential knowledge of the Trinity comes in waves, and it is in the second wave of Christian awareness that the Holy Spirit emerges from being implicitly known to being explicitly known. Divine self-revelation takes place in an act in which God is the agent who sets himself before us as someone to be known and then brings us to recognize him and then helps us understand how. We can describe it this way without even mentioning the Trinity. But to add the fully Trinitarian lens to this reality of revelation, we say more concretely that the Holy Spirit makes the Father and the Son known. True knowledge of God is knowledge of the Father and the Son by the Holy Spirit. When we describe this as happening in two steps, or coming over us in waves, we are giving a kind of temporal description of the actual spiritual structure of knowledge of the triune God.

There are several important places in Scripture that establish this pattern of beginning with focused attention on the Father and the Son while leaving the Holy Spirit in the background. Perhaps the most important one is in the middle of the Gospel of Matthew (chap. 11). At this point in his ministry, Jesus has sent out his apostles (Matt. 10:1–5) and has done conspicuous miracles in many towns, but those towns have largely rejected his message. Suddenly we are allowed to overhear Jesus praising his heavenly Father for the surprisingly uneven reception of the gospel message: "I thank you, Father, Lord of heaven and earth, that you have hidden these things from the wise and understanding and revealed them to little children; yes, Father, for such was your gracious will" (Matt. 11:25–26). What passes between Jesus and his Father here is a communication of shared joy expressed in the language of delight. Jesus confesses his full alignment with the Father's good pleasure and goes on to proclaim that "all things have been handed over to me by my Father, and no one knows the Son except the Father, and no one knows the Father except the Son and anyone to whom the Son chooses to reveal him" (Matt. 11:25–27).

What Jesus describes here is a closed circle of divine knowledge: the only one who knows the Son is the Father, and the only one who knows the Father is the Son. The only way into this circle is by the good pleasure of God, who invites people into it when the Son chooses to reveal the Father, who knows the Son, who knows the Father, who knows the Son, and so on. Around and around it goes. What else is there to say? Jesus turns immediately to the crowds (and perhaps, breaking the fourth wall of the narrative, to the reader) with a direct invitation: "Come to me, all who labor and are heavy laden, and I will give you rest" (Matt. 11:28). Jesus begins the passage talking over our heads to his Father; he ends it by talking directly to us; in between, he delivers some intense theology about knowledge of the Father and the Son, into which we are invited.

But where is the Holy Spirit?

Ignore for a moment the fact that readers have learned a few things about the Spirit already in Matthew's Gospel; he was conspicuously present at the baptism, for instance (Matt. 3:16). And ignore for a moment the fact that the risen Jesus will pick up this same way of talking about "the Father" and "the Son" in this absolute, Johannine tone of voice, in Matthew's magisterial conclusion, where he will add the name of the Holy Spirit as the only name worthy to be spoken alongside the names of the Father and the Son as the one name into which believers are to be baptized (Matt. 28:19). Set aside the Spirit's manifest presence at the Gospel's beginning and ending; the question we want to press here in Matthew 11 is, where is the Spirit? How can Jesus deliver this remarkably full exposition of the revealed knowledge of God without explicit mention of the Holy Spirit?

The answer is easy enough: Jesus knows what he is doing. The Spirit, not explicitly mentioned here, is implicitly the one in whom everything is happening. If we want to hazard a paraphrase of why Jesus did not mention the Spirit, perhaps we could say this: the main thing to say about our knowledge of God is that we know the Father in the Son, and the Son in the Father. Jesus said the main thing. We shouldn't presume to correct his theology or accuse him of ignoring the Spirit and being functionally binitarian instead of Trinitarian. Instead, we learn directly from him that being included in the knowledge the Father and Son have of each other is the primary thing. The fact that we have this knowledge in the Holy Spirit is a secondary statement, almost a statement about the statement. To speak explicitly about the Holy Spirit is to take a step back, to get more perspective on the immediate awareness of encountering the Father and the Son as they bring us into their fellowship— in the Holy Spirit.

The movement of divine revelation is never completed unless the Holy Spirit completes it. It is only in the Holy Spirit that the Son makes the Father known. But this passage doesn't say so, and there's nothing wrong with this passage. Apparently you can teach about knowing God without explicitly mentioning the Holy Spirit. Jesus did.

In the history of commenting on this passage, theologians have never concluded that the unmentioned Spirit was somehow actually absent. Thomas Aquinas (1225–1274) argues that we already needed to acknowledge the Spirit's implicit presence even when Jesus says that nobody knows the Father but the Son. "When he says here 'but the Son,' the Holy Spirit is not excluded, who is the same in nature."[8] John Calvin (1509–1564) also recognizes that giving a full theological explanation of what is happening in Matthew 11 requires naming the Holy Spirit, since "it is the Father's gift that the Son is known, for by His Spirit He opens the eyes of our minds and we perceive the glory of Christ which otherwise would be hidden from us."[9] So the Spirit is not absent from the actual event, yet he is omitted from the words of Jesus's explanation.

What is going on here? It is fair to say that throughout his ministry Jesus spoke a lot about his Father and, by proportion, relatively little about the Holy Spirit. It was his stated goal to make his Father known, not to make the Holy Spirit known. One obvious reason for this has to do with the divine timeline of revelation. Jesus was sent by the Father on his special mission, but only later, on the basis of that completed mission, would he and the Father together send the Holy Spirit. When Jesus did refer to the Spirit, John's Gospel reminds the reader

---

8. Thomas Aquinas, *Commentary on Matthew*, chap. 11, lectio 3, par. 965, https://aquinas.cc/la/en/~Matt.

9. John Calvin, *A Harmony of the Gospels Matthew, Mark, and Luke*, trans. T. H. L. Parker (Grand Rapids, MI: Eerdmans, 1995), 2:24.

that Jesus was talking in advance about what would be fulfilled later: "Now this he said about the Spirit, whom those who believed in him were to receive, for as yet the Spirit had not been given, because Jesus was not yet glorified" (John 7:39). But another reason Jesus spoke a lot about the Father and a little about the Spirit is deeper and has more to do with the particular person and work of the Spirit. The Holy Spirit is more than just the third item in chronological sequence or logical order on a list of things to be revealed; the Holy Spirit is also the active power of the revelation happening during the entire sequence.

"He Is That Person That Leadeth Us Out of Ourselves"

To switch from the language of the Gospels to the language of Paul's letters, we might put it this way: when people have faith, they call Jesus their Lord and God their Father. To call Jesus your Lord, and God your Father, is to make a robust and effective confession of faith. But these are both statements empowered by, and made sayable by, the Holy Spirit. "No one can say 'Jesus is Lord' except in the Holy Spirit" (1 Cor. 12:3), and, "You have received the Spirit of adoption as sons, by whom we cry, 'Abba! Father!'" (Rom. 8:15). It is the Holy Spirit who makes the confession of faith possible and actual, but he does not do that by making himself the object of focused attention. He does it by making Jesus and the Father the object of focused attention.

In the course of his writing ministry, Paul had good reason to give special attention to the person and work of the Holy Spirit, especially in response to church troubles and theological challenges. It is no accident that the helpful passages quoted above are from the richly pneumatological chapters of Romans 8 and 1 Corinthians 12. This special attention makes his writings a crucial help in understanding the Spirit. But the overall tendency of his teaching tracks very closely with that of Jesus; he writes a lot about Jesus and the Father, and a little about the Spirit. Paul also echoes Jesus in making strong theological statements that presuppose the Holy Spirit but leave him in the background while foregrounding the Father and the Son. Jesus and his apostles follow the same general rule, speaking always *in* the Spirit but only sometimes *of* the Spirit.

A good example of this is the way Paul characteristically begins his letters: "Grace and peace from God our Father and the Lord Jesus Christ" (Eph. 1:2). Thomas Goodwin (1600–1680) noticed the omission of the Spirit from this phrase: "Where is the Holy Spirit? Here is only God the Father and Jesus Christ mentioned . . . ; what should be the reason of that?"[10] Goodwin is glad to give two answers to his own question. Far from being embarrassed about Paul's supposed failure to mention the Holy Spirit, he draws readers into the theological depth of this characteristically biblical way of talking.

Goodwin's first answer is that when we read a passage like this, we should understand that the Holy Spirit is implicitly included: "It is not that the Holy Ghost is not the author of both these [grace and peace] as well as the Father and the Son, nor that he is not intended here in this blessing. No, the works of the Trinity are undivided. If therefore from the Father and Son, then also from the Holy Ghost."[11] The reason to assume the presence of the Holy Spirit along with the Father and the Son is that the rest of the Bible trains us to count to three in matters of divine blessing. Furthermore, Goodwin sees the same reality stated more fully and triadically in the final benediction

10. Thomas Goodwin, *An Exposition of the Epistle to the Ephesians*, vol. 1, *Works of Thomas Goodwin* (Edinburgh: James Nichol, 1861), 21. Goodwin writes eighteen dense pages on the two verses, Eph. 1:1–2.
11. Goodwin, *Epistle to the Ephesians*, 1.21.

offered by an apostle, in Revelation 1:4–5: "Grace to you and peace from him who is and who was and who is to come, and from the seven spirits who are before his throne, and from Jesus Christ."[12] Goodwin takes the Bible to be a book that has adequately informed him about the Trinity. It has taught him that God is Father, Son, and Holy Spirit, and that divine blessing comes from these three divine persons. As a commentator, he does not need to cram a fully Trinitarian reference into every place where only two of the persons are named, especially not when the Father and Son are named but the Spirit omitted.

As soon as Goodwin moves on from Ephesians 1:2 to Ephesians 1:3, he encounters again the same two (not three) names in the very next verse: "Blessed be the God and Father of our Lord Jesus Christ." But this time he does not pause to ask, "Where is the Holy Spirit?" Why not? Because he already established his point about the presence of the Spirit wherever the Father and the Son are. He already said that if a book tells you clearly that all three are present and active wherever one or two are, there is no need for the same book to repeat the same point explicitly on every occasion. For Goodwin to go out of his way to force a Spirit reference into the commentary he is writing would be to violate his own principle of interpretation. Just as he applies the principle to reading the Bible, Goodwin expects his own readers to apply it to him. Goodwin's first answer to the question, Why doesn't Paul mention the Holy Spirit? is a rule about right reading. For a reader who bears in mind what is made clear in one part of a book, that clear teaching can be silently presupposed in other parts of the book.

---

12. Goodwin, *Epistle to the Ephesians*, 1:21. The "seven spirits" of Revelation are presented mysteriously, but are rightly interpreted as an evocative way of referring to the Holy Spirit in his presence to the churches. See Brandon Smith, *The Trinity in the Book of Revelation: Seeing Father, Son, and Holy Spirit in John's Apocalypse* (Downers Grove, IL: IVP Academic, 2022), 151–65.

But Goodwin's second answer goes deeper, in the sense that it examines the actual person and work of the Spirit. The first verses of Ephesians are not an anomaly; the apostles almost never mention the Holy Spirit in the opening benedictions of any of their letters. Why?

> The reason is, because it is both his office and work to reveal and communicate this grace from the Father, and peace from the Son. Hence in deed and in truth, blessing from the Holy Ghost comes to be wished in the very praying for a communication of grace and peace from God the Father and Christ. . . . He is that Person that leadeth us out of ourselves unto the grace of God the Father, and the peace and satisfaction made by Jesus Christ. Those other two Persons are in their several works rather the objects of our faith and consolation, but the Holy Ghost is the author and efficient both of our faith on them, and comfort enjoyed in and from them.[13]

This is the normal way that Scripture works, presenting the Father and the Son as objects of attention, in the power of the Holy Spirit, who is the "author and efficient," that is to say, the origin and the effective power, of our faithful attention to them. The Spirit demonstrates his almighty power and full deity most often in his effective presentation of the other two persons of the Trinity. As Goodwin says, "We look up to God the Father as the fountain of grace; and we look up to Jesus Christ as the fountain of our peace. But we are to look at the Holy Ghost as the revealer of both these from both."[14] We never did receive grace and peace from the Father and the Son without the Spirit. The Holy Spirit was always already the

13. Goodwin, *Epistle to the Ephesians*, 21.
14. Goodwin, *Epistle to the Ephesians*, 21.

one who brought all the blessings of salvation to us. He was present and active all along, even when that presence and work remained anonymous.

The Main Work in the Main Things

We have seen that the overall pattern of scriptural revelation is that the Holy Spirit's presence becomes clear at the end of the process but then turns out to have always already been there. He sometimes seems to us to be introduced late, like some kind of an afterthought. But God has no afterthoughts. What he apparently has is unstated presuppositions, which he gladly leads us into a later awareness of. And that is how we have seen the Bible directing us to encounter the Holy Spirit, never as the Holy Afterthought but always as the Holy Presupposition.

What is crucial to grasp in this orderly revelation is that the Holy Spirit's main work is in the main things—grace and peace from the Father and the Son. It is very tempting to rush past this work of the Holy Spirit as, in Goodwin's words, "the revealer of both . . . from both" in order to move on to something specifically and uniquely true of the Spirit alone. But we must resist that temptation if we intend to take Scripture as our guide. The hunger to know the Spirit better and to understand his person and work more fully is a godly hunger and a sign of spiritual health. But not every way of indulging that hunger is godly or healthy. The Holy Spirit must be sought in a way that tracks as closely as possible with his own work. That is, he must be sought spiritually. And the center of gravity for his work is not out in some new set of information or new set of adventures beyond the Father and the Son, but in their very midst. Spiritual understanding must start from here if it is to avoid misconstruing what the Bible says about the Holy Spirit even in those passages where it singles him out and teaches directly about him.

The journey of faith into communion with the Holy Spirit does not lead away from the Father and the Son.

Sadly, there really is such a thing as a neglect of the Holy Spirit. Many churches live, and many Christians think and feel, in a way that undervalues and underappreciates the Spirit. But the first step in correcting this imbalance is to recognize that the Holy Spirit's presence and power have always been operative at the very heart of the gospel itself; that without the Holy Spirit we do not have the Father or the Son either. We meet the Holy Spirit where he is, in the central realities of Christian existence with the Father and the Son, rather than in some third, extraneous zone out beyond that center.

Thomas Goodwin, who is so eloquent on how the grace and peace that come to us from the Father through the Son only ever reach us in the Spirit as "the revealer of both . . . from both," also has much to say about the Holy Spirit in particular. The sixth volume of Goodwin's *Works*, *The Work of the Holy Ghost in our Salvation*, is an excellent and extensive treatise running to more than five hundred pages.[15] Goodwin opens that volume with a heartfelt and urgent lament: "There is a general omission in the saints of God, in their not giving the Holy Ghost that glory that is due to his person, and for his great work of salvation in us, insomuch that we have in our hearts almost lost this third person."[16] Goodwin is manifestly on the team of those who are worried about overlooking the Holy Spirit. He earnestly desires to see Christians give "a proportionable honour" to the one whose person is coessential, coequal, and coeternal with the Father and the Son, and who, in his work, "though it be last done for us, he is not behind them, nor in the glory of it inferior to

---

15. Thomas Goodwin, *The Work of the Holy Ghost in Our Salvation*, vol. 6, *The Works of Thomas Goodwin* (Edinburgh: James Nichol, 1863).
16. Goodwin, *Work of the Holy Ghost*, 3.

what they have in theirs."[17] To that end, Goodwin devotes his volume to a deep study of the Spirit, working through key passages and exploring numerous doctrinal and experiential elements of pneumatology. "The scope of this treatise," he writes, "is to set forth this work [of the Spirit] to you in the amplitude of it, to the end you may accordingly in your hearts honour this blessed and holy Spirit."[18] And his primary strategy for bringing honor to the Holy Spirit is to demonstrate that the Spirit is centrally involved in the entire work of salvation. That is, he digs deeper into the very essence of salvation and shows that everything we have from the Father and through the Son comes to us only in the Spirit:

> And indeed, no less than all that is done, or to be done in us, was left to the Holy Ghost's share, for the ultimate execution of it; and it was not left him as the refuse, it being as necessary and as great as any of theirs. But he being the last person, took his own lot of the works about our salvation, which are the last, which is to apply all, and to make all actually ours, whatever the other two had done afore for us.[19]

If our goal is to do proper justice to the Holy Spirit, the most strategic move is not to rush on to some new topic that is his special preserve; the most strategic move is to insist that he has been central to all God's works and ways all along. That is, in fact, how the Bible introduces us to the Holy Spirit, as somebody who was always already active, somebody we already know. We have been entirely under his influence if we have come to know anything about God the Father or Jesus his Son. John Stott makes the point this way: "Without the Spirit, Christian discipleship would be impossible. There can

---

17. Goodwin, *Work of the Holy Ghost*, 3–4.
18. Goodwin, *Work of the Holy Ghost*, 4.
19. Goodwin, *Work of the Holy Ghost*, 4.

be no life without the life-giver, no understanding without the Spirit of truth, no fellowship without the unity of the Spirit, no Christlikeness apart from his fruit, and no witness without his power."[20]

We might ask why. Why does the Holy Spirit do everything, but withhold direct teaching about himself until late in the history of revelation? If it is in fact God's design for us to come to full knowledge of the Trinity in this structured way, why is this his design? Why is the work of the Holy Spirit so foundational from the very beginning but left so relatively anonymous until its conclusion? Why does God do it this way?

Questions like these are good, but they are of such broad scope they are somewhat like the question, why are there two testaments in the Bible? That is, why does God bring salvation by means of a schema that first presents a promise and then presents its fulfillment? If God has something good to give, why does he present it in this extended form of making and then keeping a promise? The two-testaments question, it turns out, is not just a parallel illustration of the dynamic we are discussing but is in fact the same dynamic. The Spirit belongs to the fulfillment side of the schema: he is "the promised Holy Spirit" or "the Spirit of promise." So he is rightly associated with something eschatological, with something expected and finally received. And God apparently wants to prepare us thoroughly for the moment when the eyes of our hearts are opened and the power of the Holy Spirit dawns on us. God has so ordered his revelation that the moment of the Spirit's manifestation is not just the next interesting thing in a series, or even just the chronological last thing, but is in fact the ultimate, consummating thing that makes retroactive sense of everything and brings

20. John R. W. Stott, *The Message of Acts: The Spirit, the Church, and the World* (Downers Grove, IL: InterVarsity Press, 2020), 60.

along with it all that has gone before. The Father and the Son are ours, it turns out, only in the Spirit; and that has always already been the truth of our salvation.

God makes himself known to us with careful preparation, in a deliberate, well-ordered sequence. The Holy Spirit dawns on our awareness after spanning the Testaments, having been adumbrated before being clearly revealed, and preveniently supervising the entire process that he consummates. When we meet this person, this someone we already know, we look back on our whole course of Christian instruction and realize that our path, our experience, the Bible we read, and our knowledge of God in Christ have always already been haunted by the Holy Ghost.

2

The Holy Spirit in the Trinity

For anybody who wants to learn about the Holy Spirit, having the doctrine of the Trinity already at hand provides a great head start. Pneumatology is one part of Trinitarian theology. So the doctrine of the Trinity is a powerful advance organizer that helps us locate and explore the theology of the Holy Spirit. This chapter explains the basics of the doctrine of the Trinity and why it makes a difference in our understanding of the Holy Spirit.

There is an excellent little triangle diagram that shows the elements of the doctrine of the Trinity. Figure 2.1 is a simple version of it:[1]

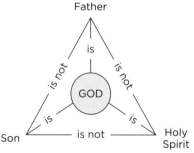

Figure 2.1

1. Nobody seems to know when the diagram originated, though it is at least as old as the twelfth century and is a straightforward representation of the first part of the Athanasian Creed.

The figure is, of course, not a drawing of the Trinity! It is instead a kind of mental map showing the key terms in the doctrine. It shows that there are three (Father, Son, and Holy Spirit) who are the one God; each of them "is God," as the lines going toward the center say. And yet each of the three is truly distinct from the others, so each of them "is not" another, as the lines going around the outside say.

The most helpful thing about figure 2.1 is that it holds before our eyes a number of truths at the same time, which enables us to keep our mental bearings as we focus on each one in turn. When it comes to the Holy Spirit, look how much we already know about the subject simply because we know that this doctrine is one part of the larger doctrine of the Trinity. The Holy Spirit, a distinct person from the Father and the Son (see the two outer lines that radiate from him), is nevertheless fully God (see his line pointing inward). He has all the attributes of deity in common with the Father and the Son but does not have fatherhood or sonship in common with them. He cannot be confused with them or separated from them. We know all this just by knowing that the Spirit is in the Trinity and that pneumatology is part of Trinitarianism.

We also know a few other important things that are, frankly, just not very well represented on this otherwise helpful ancient figure. The figure says next to nothing about the actual relations between the three persons. Technically, the only thing it tells us about their relations is negative: "not." They are not each other. That's an important point to make, since they can't be in relation to each other if they simply are each other. But it doesn't exactly warm the heart! And we know considerably more than that about the relations of Father, Son, and Holy Spirit. So we will have to let those "is not" lines stand as placeholders for now and resolve to fill them in soon with a lot more information, gleaned from Scripture. In this chapter, that will mean saying something about the main Trinitarian relations, which are the eternal relations of origin in God. But there is so much to say about the Spirit's relation to the Father on the one hand and the Spirit's relation to the Son on the other, that each of these subjects will take up a whole subsequent chapter. For now, let figure 2.1 remind us of what we already know. Consider how important it is to have an intelligent grasp of the Holy Spirit under the heading of that great, central word *God*.

The Spirit Is God

The full deity of the Holy Spirit is represented on figure 2.1 by that one little line, running from his corner of the triangle to its center. You can put your finger on it and trace the connection from the words "Holy Spirit," through the word "is," to the word "God." But when you trace that line and say that sentence, you should be aware of two things.

First, you should be aware that you're saying, in the fewest words possible, something that has to be gathered in from the message of the entire Bible about the nature of the Holy Spirit. From Genesis to Revelation, Holy Scripture speaks of the Spirit as divine. Although there is probably no place in the flow of Scripture where such a concise, down-to-business proposition like "the Holy Spirit is God" is flatly stated, there are crucial passages that make the conclusion inescapable. Consider Isaiah 63. In that passage, the prophet reminds the people of Israel how it was God himself who delivered them from Egypt when "he became their Savior" (v. 8). It was he himself "who put in the midst of them his Holy Spirit" and "who divided the waters before them to make for himself an everlasting name, who led them through the depths" (vv. 11–13). But this remembrance of their salvation comes in the middle of a prophetic rebuke, because even in the face of these great mercies, "they rebelled and grieved his Holy Spirit; therefore he turned to be their enemy" (v. 10). Notice how the Holy Spirit is named as the guarantee of God's personal presence among his people in verse 11 and also as the one who the people personally offended by their rebellion in verse 10. Isaiah looks all the way back to Exodus and identifies the Holy Spirit as the God of Israel. This passage also echoes into the New Testament, where Paul warns the Ephesians, "Do not grieve the Holy Spirit of God, by whom you were sealed for the day of redemption" (Eph. 4:30). This pancanonical proof of the Spirit's divinity is deep and wide and powerful, but one thing it is not is brief. It spans from Exodus to Ephesians. "The Holy Spirit is God" is an extremely concise way to put it, exactly what we want for a diagram such as figure 2.1. But the figure is just a memory aid that should remind you of the whole sweep of biblical revelation.

The second thing to be aware of when tracing the line "The Holy Spirit is God" is that you're pointing to something far greater than you can conceive of. One small trip with the finger is one infinite leap with the mind. To identify the Holy Spirit as God is to say that whatever God is, the Holy Spirit is. God has a nature; the Bible speaks of it as God's divinity (Rom. 1:20) or deity (Col. 2:9).[2] The King James Version translated words like these as "Godhead," a thrilling word that is basically an archaic way of saying godhood or godness. Words fail, obviously, when what we are pointing to with such words is the godness of God. But whatever godness is, it belongs to the Holy Spirit.

2. These passages use Greek words that are either a way of rendering the noun *theos*, "god," more abstract (*theotētos* in Col. 2:9), or doing the same with the adjective "divine" (*theiotēs* in Rom. 1:20). See also "the divine being" (*to theion* in Acts 17:29). Finally, Gal. 4:8 refers to idols as things that are not gods because of their nature (*physei mē ousin theois*).

When we say that the Holy Spirit is God, we mean that he is absolutely God, God without exceptions or reservations. We attribute to him everything that true divinity entails. He is not just one part of God, not even "the Spirit part of God." We may sometimes speak that way, loosely, but a moment's thought reminds us that it simply won't do to think of Father, Son, and Holy Spirit as parts. The persons of the Trinity are not fractional subsections of God. The Spirit, therefore, is not a fraction of God! As the ancient Athanasian Creed admonishes us, when we talk about the Trinity we should take care not to disassemble the divine substance into segments, not even into thirds. "We worship one God in Trinity, and Trinity in Unity, neither confounding the Persons, nor dividing the Substance," says the creed. The Father, Son, and Holy Spirit are distinct persons, but "the Godhead of the Father, of the Son, and of the Holy Spirit, is all one, the Glory equal, the Majesty co-eternal."[3]

That word "co-eternal" is powerfully constructed. It takes a divine attribute (eternity) and joins to it the prefix *co-*, making it a compact statement of the doctrine of the triune God. You could pick any divine attribute that comes to mind and put the prefix *co-* on it to show how it is shared fully among the three. They are not only coeternal, but also co-omnipotent, co-omniscient, comerciful, and so on. This is because they are coessential, having the same divine essence. Every divine attribute follows the same rules rehearsed in the Athanasian Creed:

> The Father uncreated, the Son uncreated, and the Holy Spirit uncreated. The Father incomprehensible, the Son incomprehensible, and the Holy Spirit incomprehensible. The

3. Chad Van Dixhoorn, *Creeds, Confessions, and Catechisms: A Reader's Edition* (Wheaton, IL: Crossway, 2022), 19.

Father eternal, the Son eternal, and the Holy Spirit eternal. And yet they are not three eternals, but one eternal. As also there are not three incomprehensibles, nor three uncreated, but one uncreated, and one incomprehensible.

So likewise the Father is Almighty, the Son Almighty, and the Holy Spirit Almighty. And yet they are not three Almighties, but one Almighty. So the Father is God, the Son is God, and the Holy Spirit is God. And yet they are not three Gods, but one God. So likewise the Father is Lord, the Son Lord, and the Holy Spirit Lord. And yet there are not three Lords, but one Lord.

All of this is telescoped into the one line on figure 2.1 that runs from "Holy Spirit" to "God." This is the first and most obvious way that knowing the doctrine of the Trinity gives us our bearings for the doctrine of the Holy Spirit.

The Spirit Is in God

But we can say something more about the Holy Spirit. Not only is he God, but he is also *in* God. There is something about the Holy Spirit that makes it especially proper to say that he is interior to God, deep inside of divinity, dwelling within the divine life in its depths. Already when we talk about the Spirit as the breath of God, we are following Scripture by saying that he comes forth similar to the way breath comes forth from inside of a creature. And along with this respiratory image, Scripture gives us another one, even more clearly emphasizing this interiority. Paul asks, "Who knows a person's thoughts except the spirit of that person, which is in him? So also no one comprehends the thoughts of God except the Spirit of God" (1 Cor. 2:11). Paul is drawing an analogy here. Just like your own spirit is so deep within you that it is intimate with your own thoughts in a way that nobody outside of you could possibly be, so it is with God. God's own Spirit is inside of God. Nothing in God is hidden from the Spirit of God, because the Spirit is God, and is also somehow in God.

What more can we say about what it means for the Spirit to be in God? This is the very definition of a deep subject, and it would make sense if we simply had to acknowledge that Scripture points to it as true and then lay our hand over our mouth and move on in silence. But Scripture draws out at least a few implications. One is simply that the Spirit being *in* God forms the background of the Spirit being *from* God. He comes forth from within; as we rejoice that he is from God, we should rejoice that he is in God.

But a second implication is more directly practical. After informing us that the Spirit of God knows what is in God, Paul assures us that "we have received . . . the Spirit who is from God, that we might understand the things freely given us by God" (1 Cor. 2:12). The kind of knowledge of God that we receive in Christ is not simply a transfer of a certain set of facts or information. It is something more than that, precisely because it is brought about by the Spirit who is in God becoming the Spirit of God in us; when believers receive the Holy Spirit, they receive an understanding of what is in God. In this passage from 1 Corinthians, the Holy Spirit is identified with the kind of knowledge of God that goes to the very heart of who God is—the depths, the deep things of God—and at the same time with a kind of knowledge that is not reserved for scholars and those who have achieved the wisdom of the world but is given by God to the simple and to those who are accounted, by worldly standards, fools. The Spirit stands behind an encounter with God that is definitely cognitive, explicitly about knowledge. And it is a knowledge that is special and reserved, but not reserved for the elite; it is reserved for those who receive it from God, by the Spirit whom God gives from himself. To receive the Holy Spirit is to be plunged into the depths of the knowledge of God.

Scottish theologian Robert Rollock (1555–1599) gave a striking exposition of why it matters that the Spirit who is in God is the one who makes us know God. "Look what more the Spirit does," says Rollock.

> He is not content to take the veil from thy heart; but he takes thy soul by the hand, as it were, and leads it in through the deepness—["the deep things"]—of God. He will ravish it out of the body, as it were, and lead it into that light that has no access—["the light that is inaccessible"];—and he will say: Lo! there is the mercy; Lo! There is the righteousness; Lo! there is the everlasting life that is spoken of. Seest thou not them all in him? Thus will he point out everything in God.[4]

And in order to "make the matter more plain," Rollock even engages in a thought experiment. Imagine, he says, that "my spirit or soul entered into thee." What would happen?

> If my spirit or my soul be in thee, there would be nothing within me but thou wouldst see it; all my thoughts would be patent to thee. Now to apply this. This is no supposition: God will put his Spirit in us. For if his Spirit be not in us, woe be to us for ever. If God put his Spirit in us, must it not follow of necessity that we must see in God, at least the things that concern our weal and salvation. That Spirit in me—in thee—must reveal to me—to thee—the things that

---

4. I quote this, including the bracketed sections, from the version given in Hugh Martin, who has rendered Robert Rollock's Scottish writing into easier English (Hugh Martin, *Christ's Presence in the Gospel History* [London: T. Nelson & Sons, 1860], 182). Rollock's phrasing in the original is incredibly powerful but distracting for most readers ("luik quhat mair the Spreit dois"). Find it in *The Select Works of Robert Rollock*, ed. William M. Gunn (Edinburgh: The Woodrow Society, 1849), 1:385.

lie in the very deepness of God which concern our weal and salvation. And that man that has the Spirit of God will see the very heart of God and his mind. He will see the remission of his sins in the mind of God; and all, by the benefit of the Spirit of Jesus that dwells in him. So we have a great advantage here; that, by the benefit of the Spirit, we see the things that are in God.[5]

As surely as the breath is in your chest, as deeply as the thoughts lie in your mind, the Spirit is in God. And his being in God is the guarantee that the knowledge he brings to us comes from the heart of God.

It is typical of the Bible's way of teaching that we really only learn this exalted and mysterious truth about the Holy Spirit when we learn about how it applies to us. That is, Scripture is most clear about the Spirit's existence inside of God when it is most serious about telling us why that matters to us. God is not generally in the business of telling us various fascinating and astonishing things about himself simply in the abstract, and is never in the business of merely satisfying our curiosity or puffing us up with knowledge. "The secret things belong to the LORD our God, but the things that are revealed belong to us and to our children forever, that we may do all the words of this law" (Deut. 29:29). Among the things that God has revealed to us is that his Holy Spirit, who is in him, enters into us to give us understanding. Of course much remains mysterious, and even in showing us these deep things, God still reserves his sovereign secrecy as the incomprehensible God—the Father incomprehensible, the Son incomprehensible, and the Holy Spirit incomprehensible—yet there are not three incomprehensibles but one.

5. Martin, *Christ's Presence*, 183.

The Spirit Is from God:
Eternal Procession and Temporal Mission

The doctrine of the Trinity has provided a helpful framework for confessing that the Holy Spirit is God and even that the Spirit is in God, although it would have been possible to confess both of these things without making any direct appeal to the doctrine of the Trinity. But a Trinitarian approach to these pneumatological truths has laid a foundation for us now to say something about the Holy Spirit that is necessarily Trinitarian, something that directly appeals to the eternal relations of Father, Son, and Holy Spirit. What we need to say next is that the Holy Spirit is *from* God. For understanding the Holy Spirit, the *fromness* is everything.

The most obvious sense in which the Holy Spirit is from God is that God sent the Spirit. To be specific, God prophetically promised to send his Spirit (Joel 2) in the fullness of time and then fulfilled that promise (Acts 2). When the disciples broke out in multilingual praise of the mighty works of God, Peter explained that the second chapter of Joel was happening in the second chapter of Acts (so to speak). Recounting the gospel story, he concluded by saying that Jesus, having been "exalted at the right hand of God, and having received from the Father the promise of the Holy Spirit, . . . has poured out this that you yourselves are seeing and hearing" (Acts 2:33). On the day of Pentecost, on the basis of the finished work of Christ, the Father and the Son sent the Holy Spirit (John 14:16, 26; 15:26; 16:7) to indwell believers, to be a source of life within them, and to empower them to testify about Jesus. Since that great epochal inbreaking of the Spirit, he now comes from God to us, sent into our hearts and enabling us to call God our Father (Gal. 4:6). This all-important, salvation-historical sending of the Holy Spirit is an event on the timeline of God's well-ordered plan. Together with the incarnation of the Son, the outpouring of the Holy Spirit occupies the very center of salvation history. We will have more to say about this great event in later chapters, especially in its relation to the Father (chapter 3) and the Son (chapter 4). For now, we simply need to acknowledge it as the central, visible mission of the Holy Spirit, the most obvious way that he is from God.

But the Holy Spirit has a deeper fromness than his sending. There is a fromness that he would have had even if there had never been an outpouring of the Spirit in Acts 2. Behind the sending of the Spirit into salvation history stands the eternal procession of the Holy Spirit within the life of God. In fact, the salvation-historical fromness depends on the eternal, internal fromness, and manifests it for us. On the basis of the Spirit's sending, we can recognize that even within the life of God, the third person is eternally from the Father. Recall the two biblical images we have been using to help grasp the Holy Spirit's identity: the Holy Spirit is like breath, and the Holy Spirit is like a creature's own internal spirit by which a creature knows its own thoughts. In both cases, these are images of things that come forth from somebody. Breath comes forth out of a breather, and the knowledge of an internal spirit comes out from a creature who expresses what is in him. In both cases, the fact that something comes out from a source entails that it was already living and active inside. In fact, in both images we can dimly see that there was not only something inside, but something going on inside. There was something going around or circulating in there. It would be even better to say that there was something already "going forth" without ever coming out. It was internal procession. Breath was already a kind of emanating life, even within the chest of the breather, and the internal spirit was already reaching out to its own internal self-understanding without leaving its own sphere of intelligent life and love. Using the image of breath, we could say there was eternal spirating within the life of God; using the image of intelligent spirit, we could say it was always intelligently, vitally spiritual.

In the case of the Holy Spirit, Christian doctrine has traditionally described his eternal existence as an eternal procession, or relation of origin, from the Father. Just as God the Son eternally subsists as the one who is eternally begotten or generated from God the Father, so God the Holy Spirit eternally subsists as the one eternally spirated or proceeding from God the Father.[6] We should say briefly here that the Spirit eternally comes *at least* from God the Father, since the Western churches have traditionally wanted to add, "and also from the Son," while the Eastern churches have definitely denied this. We will address that disagreement in more detail below. For now it will be enough to affirm that the Spirit proceeds from the Father in such a way that he is also eternally connected to the Son: "The Eternal Son is no stranger to the procession of the Holy Spirit."[7] We say that the Spirit proceeds from the Father, not from the Breather or the Spirator. That is, the first person ("Father") is already characterized by his relation to the second person ("of the Son") before we speak of him as the source of the third person ("Spirit"). So to proceed from the Father is to be somehow (we can be vague for now) marked also by the

---

6. On the eternal generation of the Son, see Fred Sanders and Scott Swain, eds., *Retrieving Eternal Generation* (Grand Rapids, MI: Zondervan, 2016). For recent evangelical treatments of the Spirit's procession, see Scott Swain, *The Trinity: An Introduction* (Wheaton, IL: Crossway, 2020), 89–103. See also Gregg R. Allison and Andreas J. Köstenberger, *The Holy Spirit* (Nashville, TN: B&H, 2020), 255–64.

7. Boris Bobrinskoy, *The Mystery of the Trinity: Trinitarian Experience and Vision in the Biblical and Patristic Tradition* (Crestwood, NY: St. Vladimir's Seminary Press, 1999), 302. I quote an Eastern Orthodox theologian here intentionally, to indicate that both traditions, in their own ways, gladly confess that the Spirit is "the Spirit of the Son" eternally; Bobrinskoy emphasizes the "reciprocal concomitance" of Son and Spirit. See his whole treatment of the subject, 274–303.

Son.[8] The result of this is that the Holy Spirit is rightly named third in a sequence that follows after the Father first and the Son second. And he brings with him, on his special mission into salvation history, his origin from the Father and the Son.

Our purpose here is only to get a clear view of the truth that the Holy Spirit is eternally from God, within God, as God. We need this clear view so that we can recognize how his temporal mission in salvation history is grounded in his eternal procession within the life of God. The Holy Spirit comes forth among us for our salvation in a way that corresponds to the way he proceeds from the Father within the divine life. There is a revealed connection between the Spirit's procession and his mission. Indeed, "the structure of the Holy Spirit's mission displays or exhibits the fundamental structure of his eternal procession."[9]

In light of the eternal procession of the Spirit, we can now look back on what we called the mission of the Spirit and be more precise about it. Recall the two *fromnesses* that we started with. The Father sent the Spirit, and that mission was based on an eternal procession. When we use the word *mission* in this way, we are using it as a very special, even technical term in Trinitarian theology. It's not just any sending but precisely a sending that does what this one does: it makes known in history the eternal procession in God. When we use the word *mission* in this sense, we really have two main things in mind, and they are the two most important events in salvation history: the mission of the Son in the incarnation and the mission of the Holy Spirit at Pentecost. These are the two sendings that make known the

8. Readers who reject the *filioque* will need to bear with the fact that the shape of my argument is broadly Western, and runs most smoothly for readers who assume that the Spirit proceeds from the Father and the Son. But see the end of chap. 3 for some significant concessions more hospitable for antifilioquist sensibilities.

9. Gilles Emery, *The Trinitarian Theology of Saint Thomas Aquinas*, trans. Francesca Aran Murphy (Oxford, UK: Oxford University Press, 2007), 272.

two eternal processions in the life of God. These are, in fact, the two ways that God is with us precisely as he exists in himself. The eternal Son's mission means taking up human nature and being the incarnate Son among us, while the eternal Holy Spirit's mission means indwelling redeemed human nature on the basis of the finished atonement. In both cases, we confess that God is with us, as Immanuel and as the one who indwells his people. This is our experience of the Trinity in the history of salvation: the Father sends the Son, and Father and Son send the Holy Spirit.[10]

Despite these sallies into Trinitarian theology, this is not a book about the Trinity. It is a short introduction to the Holy Spirit. But as we have seen, our doctrine of the Trinity must be up and running before we can make our way through the doctrine of the Holy Spirit. Our understanding of the Holy Spirit will be dangerously decontextualized unless we can locate it within the doctrine of the Trinity. We might have an insecure grasp of the Bible's message about the Holy Spirit unless we see that he is God, in God, from God. All of this must be established before we can hope to make sense out of what he does. Unless we recognize the eternal, Trinitarian depth of his being and his personhood, we run the risk of losing him in his own work; that is, we could start at the wrong end of the doctrine and reduce the Holy Spirit to a set of vaguely divine effects produced among God's people by God-in-general. We might even mistake the Spirit for a way of talking about the Father in dynamic action, or about the Son working beyond his incarnation. But having secured the Trinitarian matrix of the Spirit's identity, we can safely move on to the field of the Holy Spirit's work.

10. For a longer account of this, see Fred Sanders, *The Triune God* (Grand Rapids, MI: Zondervan, 2016), 93–144.

The Spirit Works Inseparably with the Father and the Son

As we turn from the person of the Holy Spirit to his work, let us recall what we are doing. Our goal is to understand the deep background of the Holy Spirit's work so that we can know him more fully when we encounter him in that work. We are deliberately taking an indirect route to knowledge of the Spirit, setting it in the context of the full doctrine of the Trinity. It may feel like a detour, but we will gain a tremendous amount of perspective, and the result will be a deeper understanding of the Spirit's work.

The most important thing to say about the work of the Holy Spirit is that it is inseparable from the work of the Father and the Son. His work is always radically united to the work of the whole Trinity and yet is truly his own work. Traditionally we describe this radical unity using the doctrine of the inseparable operations of the Trinity. This doctrine is worth paying attention to because when the triune God does anything, it is in some ways similar to creaturely work but is different from creatures in a more fundamental way. I want to warn you that this doctrine's somewhat intimidating name reflects the fact that the doctrine itself is counterintuitive enough to be mind-blowing.

The starting point for the doctrine of inseparable operations is easy enough. In fact, it is even fun for anybody who enjoys Bible study. It begins when you notice that Scripture consistently ascribes the same divine works to all three persons of the Trinity. Creation, for instance, is ascribed to the Father, his Word, and his Breath (Job 33:4; Pss. 33:6; 100:3; 102:26–28; John 1:3). Or consider a vital event like the resurrection of Christ. Scripture tells us that the Father raised him up (1 Cor. 6:14), that the Son had power to raise himself up (John 2:19), and that the Spirit quickened him (1 Pet. 3:18). All resurrection from the dead, in fact, is accomplished by the Father (John 5:21), the Son (also John 5:21), and the Holy Spirit (John 6:63). The Father sanctifies (Jude 1), the Son sanctifies (Heb. 2:11), and the Holy Spirit sanctifies (Rom. 15:16).[11] You may notice that this doctrine has to be assembled from many distinct passages of Scripture, because the Bible has different reasons for identifying Father, Son, and Holy Spirit as active in these works in different contexts. But the result, after just a little bit of cross-referencing and collation, is a recognition that Father, Son, and Holy Spirit are each identified as the ones carrying out the same exact actions. That is already saying a lot about their indivisible operations.

In everything they do, Father, Son, and Holy Spirit work in unison. But their cooperation is so uniquely intimate that we probably shouldn't even call it cooperation, technically. There aren't three different operations coordinated with each other, after all. Consider the human analogy of three workers. When three people work together on a project, each does his own part of it. As Gregory of Nyssa (335–395) describes it, "even if several are engaged in the same form of action, [they] work separately each by himself at the task he has undertaken, having no participation in his individual action with others who are engaged in the same occupation." There are distances between them and differences between them. They take turns (which is a kind of distance in time), or work on different parts of the project (distance in space), or come to the project from different angles (again, from different spaces). "Each of them is sepa-

---

11. Most of these correspondences are taken from William Jones of Nayland, *The Catholic Doctrine of a Trinity* (1756; repr., Philadelphia: D. Dickinson, 1818), 170–74. Nayland's book is a remarkable demonstration of the Trinity by way of extensive cross-referencing. It inspired Charles Wesley to write over a hundred hymns on the Trinity, closely following Nayland's references. For a concise collection of passages that include the Holy Spirit in divine works, see Zacharias Ursinus, *Commentary on the Heidelberg Catechism* (1852; repr., Phillipsburg, NJ: Presbyterian & Reformed, 1992), 275.

rated from the others within his own environment, according to the special character of his operation."[12]

But none of these differences apply to the Trinity. The reason Nyssa spent time itemizing the nature of cooperation is so he could explain that Father, Son, and Holy Spirit don't work together in that way:

> But in the case of the Divine nature we do not similarly learn that the Father does anything by Himself in which the Son does not work conjointly, or again that the Son has any special operation apart from the Holy Spirit; but every operation which extends from God to the Creation, and is named according to our variable conceptions of it, has its origin from the Father, and proceeds through the Son, and is perfected in the Holy Spirit. For this reason the name derived from the operation is not divided with regard to the number of those who fulfil it, because the action of each concerning anything is not separate and peculiar, but whatever comes to pass . . . comes to pass by the action of the Three, yet what does come to pass is not three things.[13]

This is a classic statement of the inseparable external operations of the Trinity.[14] Athanasius of Alexandria (296–373) taught that "the Father does all things through the Word and in the Holy Spirit. In this way is the unity of the Holy Trinity preserved."[15] Gregory of Nyssa drew out this line of thought a bit more explicitly by saying that "every operation . . . has its

12. Gregory of Nyssa, "Not Three Gods," in *Nicene and Post-Nicene Fathers*, ed. Henry Schaff and Philip Wace, series 2, vol. 5 (New York: Charles Scribner's Sons, 1917), 331–36.

13. Gregory of Nyssa, "Not Three Gods, " 334.

14. For a full-length account, see Adonis Vidu, *The Same God Who Works All Things: Inseparable Operations in Trinitarian Theology* (Grand Rapids, MI: Eerdmans, 2021).

15. Athanasius of Alexandria, "Letters to Serapion" (1.28.2–3), in *Works on the Spirit: Athanasius the Great and Didymus the Blind*, trans. Mark DelCogliano, Andrew Radde-Gallwitz, and Lewis Ayres (Crestwood, NY: St. Vladimir's Seminary Press, 2011), 97.

origin from the Father, and proceeds through the Son, and is perfected in the Holy Spirit." Each of these operations manifests a single divine power coming forth from the divine nature. Each of these actions that "extends from God to the Creation" is a work in which Father, Son, and Spirit work indivisibly, but according to the order "from the Father . . . through the Son . . . in the Holy Spirit."[16] That order is carried over from the internal life of God so that it is reflected in the external works. So each divine work is inseparably the work of all three persons in unison, though we can recognize each of them in it. We recognize them not by the differences or distances in their ways of working but by the repetition of their eternal order, which we can indicate prepositionally: from the Father, through the Son, in the Spirit. From, through, in.

Inserting this from-through-in dynamic into each act of God may seem like an unnecessary complication when all you want to say is that God did something, but it's actually very helpful. It calls back to mind that everything God does happens from the Father, through the Son, and in the Spirit. And this is more or less what you might expect is going on in divine actions anyway, given the deep oneness of God in Father, Son, and Spirit. According to Gregory of Nyssa, if you had three different actions and counted backward along that line to three different operations that produced them collaboratively, you would have no reason to suspect a single divine nature behind it all. Instead, you would have some pretty good evidence that three different gods were at work, even if they were working together. If, on the other hand, you knew that the Father begets the Son, and that the Spirit proceeds from the Father of the Son, then it would make sense to say that that eternal order of oneness would also be reflected in their way of working, when

16. Athanasius, "Letters to Serapion," 97.

they work an external act in which they are inseparable but not indistinguishable. Starting from God's Trinitarian way of being, you would already know to be on the lookout for this Trinitarian way of working. And it's not just any Trinitarian way of working (as if you could chop up a single work into three phases and assign them to three persons), but the same Trinitarian pattern we have already rehearsed: from the Father, through the Son, in the Spirit.

The doctrine of the inseparable operations of the Trinity makes deep sense with how the Bible talks about the work of Father, Son, and Holy Spirit. It rescues us from misinterpreting God's actions in two erroneous ways. First, if we are tempted to flatten out all of God's works as if God's oneness made triunity irrelevant, then inseparable operations reminds us to think harder about how every divine work truly involves Father, Son, and Holy Spirit. Second, if we are tempted to think of the three persons of the Trinity as three separate agents who are merely collaborating on a shared project from different angles, this doctrine reminds us that their unity must be deeper than that. This reminder is especially medicinal for our understanding of the Holy Spirit's work. It's fair to say that when we divide up the works of the Trinity, our understanding of the Spirit suffers first and most. We tend to ignore his participation in the work done by the Father and the Son, and we tend to isolate him in his own work. The from-through-in structure of inseparable Trinitarian action comes to the rescue. When we say (rightly!) that the Father is the Creator of heaven and earth, the doctrine of inseparable operations reminds us to open our minds to the fuller, deeper truth that creation is from the Father, through the Son, and in the Holy Spirit. When we praise the Son (rightly!) for saving us, we recall that this salvation originates with the Father, works through the Son, and is perfected in the Holy Spirit. In other words, inseparable operations reminds us not to leave out the Holy Spirit from any divine action. Conversely, when we confess (rightly!) that the Holy Spirit indwells us, the doctrine of inseparable operations reminds us that the indwelling is from the Father, through the Son. In other words, inseparable operations reminds us not to single out the Holy Spirit and make his work seem disconnected. The work of the Spirit is always the same work that begins with the Father and proceeds through the Son, being perfected in the Holy Spirit.

Some Divine Actions Are Appropriately Appropriated

If everything God does is an indivisible action coming from the Father, through the Son, and in the Holy Spirit, why are there certain divine actions that the Bible seems to go out of its way to ascribe to one particular person? Even when we carry out the cross-referencing exercise that shows Father, Son, and Holy Spirit all doing the same single action, why does one particular person sometimes predominate over the others as the one who seems to be especially responsible for it? Why does the Apostles' Creed, for instance, summarize the witness of Scripture by saying that we believe in God the Father almighty as the maker of heaven and earth? Why do we say that God the Father so loved the world that he sent his only Son? Why do we say that the Son of God accomplishes redemption and the Holy Spirit applies it? As great as the doctrine of inseparable operations is, it can sometimes feel as if it threatens to empty out our ability to talk about the persons of the Trinity doing anything in particular. And since those ways of talking are definitely grounded in the very words of Scripture, it is imperative that we don't let any theological ideas loom up as constructs that come between us and the Bible. Fortunately, the conflict here is only apparent, not real. Inseparable operations is itself a doctrine gathered from Scripture, as we have seen.

There are two main reasons that Scripture assigns certain particular divine works to particular persons of the Trinity. The first reason takes us back to the crucial doctrine of processions. Recall that there are some divine actions that are actual missions of the Son and the Holy Spirit. The incarnation of the Son is the Father sending the Son into the world in a way that manifests his eternal generation. And the outpouring of the Holy Spirit at Pentecost is the Father sending the Spirit into the church on the basis of the Son's finished work. These are special cases in which the whole point is to make the persons of the Trinity personally present and effectively known to us. Even in these cases, we can still say that there is a certain inseparability to the work since the Son only becomes incarnate as the one sent from the Father into a body prepared by the Holy Spirit (Luke 1:35). But it is only the Son who is sent. Only the Son is incarnate, even though the incarnation of the Son is the work of the whole Trinity.[17] And something parallel is true for the Holy Spirit: Pentecost is his special, personal mission into salvation history, making known his own eternal procession within the life of God. So while all the actions and works that happened around Pentecost (rushing wind, tongues of flame, and so on) were the work of the entire Trinity, still the mission itself was the mission of the Holy Spirit alone. The missions of the Son and the Spirit are utterly special.

But there is a second reason why Scripture ascribes particular actions to particular persons of the Trinity, even in cases where the action ascribed is one of those common actions that

17. The doctrine of the incarnation of the Son is one I wish I had space here to explore, but to do so would definitely be to move away from the doctrine of the Holy Spirit. For more on the missions, see Adonis Vidu, *The Divine Missions: An Introduction* (Eugene, OR: Cascade, 2022).

we have described as inseparable operations. God has chosen to use certain actions as opportunities to show us what the distinct persons of the Trinity are like. He has chosen some historical actions in the world that are instructively similar to the eternal, internal order of subsistence in the Trinity and has habitually associated those actions with the corresponding persons. Remember that the internal order of subsistence is from the Father, through the Son, in the Holy Spirit, and that this order is manifested in a corresponding from-through-in structure in the outer works. It is because of this correspondence that God tends to appropriate certain actions to certain persons.

Because it focuses on things that are appropriate in this way, this doctrine is called "appropriation." It picks out divine actions that, while not the exclusive work of one person of the Trinity, are instructively similar to a particular person of the Trinity. The great creedal example is that we confess God the Father to be maker of heaven and earth, not properly, exclusively, or in isolation from the Son and the Spirit, but by appropriation. The coming forth of all things from the one God is instructively like the coming forth of the Son and the Spirit from the Father in the divine life. Most appropriations yield their secrets to the application of the formula "from the Father, through the Son, in the Spirit." Common divine actions in which origin is prominent cluster around the Father; actions in which God accomplishes his plan cluster around the Son; actions in which created things are finalized cluster around the Spirit. In a fully formed Trinitarian reading of Scripture, numerous statements about Father, Son, and Spirit that strike us as being exclusive to them, on closer consideration, turn out to be statements employing appropriation. We pay close attention to them because we ought to; God intends to instruct us in something distinctly true about the appropriated person. Appropriation is not just a word game, but a divinely guided way of recognizing and knowing a particular person of the Trinity.

In slightly more technical language, appropriation is defined as "a process . . . by which certain absolute divine attributes and operations, which are essentially common to the entire Trinity, are ascribed to one of the Divine Persons in particular, with the purpose of revealing the Hypostatic character of that Person."[18] The main rule that governs how appropriation can be used is that, positively, there has to be some kind of intrinsic similarity between the action and the person. Negatively, we need to remember that appropriation is never exclusive to that appropriated person of the Trinity. In fact, that person of the Trinity is not even comparatively more responsible for the appropriated action. Just because we appropriate creation to the Father, we do not exclude the Son and the Spirit, or even think that somehow the Father is more especially the Creator. Appropriation is never about shutting out the other Trinitarian persons; it is about using a common work to pick out the manner of subsisting that is especially characteristic of one.[19]

We have been given a lot of distinctions to follow. It can feel like whiplash to have to bear in mind not only inseparable operations but then also appropriations. The first move seems to lump the persons of the Trinity together more than we are used to, while the second seems to take them apart again, but not really. Especially if these are new ideas to you, you may need to devote a little bit of time not just to becoming reassured that they are scripturally grounded but also to simply digesting

18. Joseph Pohle and Arthur Preuss, *The Divine Trinity: A Dogmatic Treatise by Joseph Pohle*, ed. Arthur Preuss (St. Louis: B. Herder, 1930), 244. Notice that Pohle-Preuss extends the use of appropriation to include not just works but divine attributes. This is correct, but for our discussion of the Holy Spirit we are mainly concerned with works.

19. More details can be found in Aquinas, *Summa Theologiae* 1a Q39, art. 7; and John Owen, *Communion with the Triune God*, ed. Kelly M. Kapic and Justin Taylor (Wheaton, IL: Crossway, 2007), 89–107.

them. The goal is to be able to use these doctrines smoothly and fluently for reading the Bible well and recognizing the Holy Spirit more deeply for who he is and what he does.

To Him Belongs the Consummation of All Things

It is this final move, of appropriating to the Holy Spirit the final application of salvation, that we want to focus on as our final step in the project of locating the Holy Spirit within the Trinity. When we think about the Holy Spirit in full biblical and Trinitarian perspective, we should learn to associate him and his work with the conclusion, completion, and perfecting of all God's work. This has a parallel in how we think of the Father. We should learn to start our thinking about God the Father by recognizing him as the origin of all things, so that creation itself is a giant visual aid reminding us that the Father is the primal source of the divine life itself. Similarly, we should learn to conclude our thinking about God the Spirit by recognizing him as the goal and completion toward which all things move so that the consummation of creaturely history itself is a giant visual aid reminding us that the Spirit is the perfection of the triune life itself.

To think of the Holy Spirit as the consummating person is to entertain a very large thought. One way of getting a grip on it is suggested by Petrus van Mastricht (1630–1706). Mastricht knew that the Holy Spirit "has the third place" in the Trinitarian order for two related reasons. First, in "the order and mode of subsisting," he subsists from the Father and the Son. And then in the "mode of operating," he operates from the Father and the Son. The important truth that this shows about the Spirit is that "just as he subsists, he also operates."[20]

---

20. *sicut subsistit, ita etiam operatur.* Petrus van Mastricht, *Theoretico-Practical Theology*, vol. 2, *Faith in the Triune God* (Grand Rapids, MI: Reformation Heritage, 2019), 567.

So we start at the highest level of Trinitarian affirmation: the Holy Spirit is God but is a particular person or hypostasis of God. That personal existence, or subsistence, is in God in a particular, relational way—eternally from the Father and the Son. Subsisting in that way, as third, he also operates in that way. But in this context, when Mastricht says *operate*, he is not yet talking about an outward work of the Trinity. *Operation* is a broad enough term that it can also refer to an inward, eternal operation. That inward operation is of course something we already know about; it grounds the order of subsistence, meaning it aligns with the eternal relation of proceeding from the Father and the Son. All of this (origin, subsistence, operation) is at the level of the eternal, internal, essential life of the triune God.

But the next step is a step toward us creatures by the Holy Spirit: "From these truths, to him belongs by economic office the consummation of things, namely regeneration, conversion, sanctification, and so forth."[21] The way the Spirit subsists in God shows up in the way the Holy Spirit carries out the divine works of redemption. Just as he is third, or we might say, final, in the eternal order of perfect deity, so he behaves thirdly or finally in the work of God. "To him belongs by economic office the consummation of things."

Of course this only works because we already have our theology of the inseparable outward works of the Trinity up and running. Whatever God does, the whole Trinity does. So when we hear that consummation belongs to the Holy Spirit, we shouldn't imagine that the Father and the Son ran the first two laps of the race and then passed the baton to the Holy Spirit for the third lap. Instead, we should recognize the Spirit as the one who works inseparably with the Father and the Son but always with the personal characteristic that we have to call

21. Mastricht, *Theoretico-Practical Theology*, 2:567.

"thirdness." When the works of God are coming to a perfect conclusion and consummating (as in regeneration, conversion, and sanctification), the Spirit is operating there as he subsists: from the Father and through the Son as the final one within every act. And so the acts that shine forth most clearly as consummations are the acts in which the particular character of the Holy Spirit shines forth as well. He operates as he subsists, and the consummation of things belongs to him by economic office.

We might put it this way: just as we appropriate creation to the Father, we appropriate eschatology to the Holy Spirit. In neither case are we excluding the other persons of the Trinity, or denying inseparable operations. But just think how much context and orientation this gives us for a deeper understanding of the Holy Spirit. It grounds his particular personhood in the eternal relations of God and casts all his work into the form of consummation and completion. It sets us up to find him everywhere, without losing his particular personal identity. Locating the Holy Spirit in the Trinity not only preserves us from a number of errors (like separating or confusing the persons), but more positively, it sets pneumatology in a comprehensive context that explains all of God's work from the point of view of final perfection.

John Owen makes the same point, in equally expansive language: "Whereas the order of operation among the distinct persons depends on the order of their subsistence in the blessed Trinity, in every great work of God, the concluding, completing, perfecting acts are ascribed unto the Holy Ghost."[22] The Holy Spirit ties everything together in salvation history because he is, in this history as he is within the eternal life of the Trinity, the completion.

22. John Owen, *Pneumatologia*, in *The Works of John Owen*, ed. William H. Gould (1674; repr., Edinburgh: Banner of Truth, 1967), 3:94.

Knowing the Spirit as consummator has many implications for our understanding of the message of Scripture, and we will see them unfold in the remaining chapters. But as we conclude this chapter on the Spirit in the Trinity, we should notice how much our biblical theology is enriched by giving attention to the triune God's own life. Scholars who specialize in tracing the historical lines of biblical theology have pointed out how important the Holy Spirit is for the doctrine of eschatology. The consummation of world history is a field charged with the reality of the Spirit.[23] This is a thrilling theme for Bible study, but it is even more significant when we recognize how the eschatological shape of God's work in history is grounded in the dynamics of the Trinitarian life proper, above and beyond all worldly history. The Bible appropriates eschatology and consummation to the Holy Spirit because of who he is as third in the Trinity.

With teachers like Mastricht and Owen, we have been making use of scholastic theology in its Protestant form. As is often the case with theology operating in scholastic mode, we have gathered together a lot of concepts and learned to make some careful distinctions. We call in such writers specifically when we need that kind of work done. They have the sharpest tools and the strongest supporting structures. It can seem like a long way around when our only goal is to get insight into the character of the Holy Spirit's person and work. But having traveled this road, we are in a position to reapproach the Bible with an enriched understanding of the eternal background behind the Spirit's temporal works so that we can see much more in what it says about the work of the Holy Spirit.

---

23. Geerhardus Vos, "The Eschatological Aspect of the Pauline Conception of the Spirit," in *Biblical and Theological Studies* (New York: Charles Scribner's Sons, 1912). See also Neill Q. Hamilton, *The Holy Spirit and Eschatology in Paul* (Edinburgh: Oliver & Boyd, 1957).

3

The Holy Spirit and
the Father

The Holy Spirit is often considered the person of the Trinity most in danger of being neglected or ignored. We certainly ought to be vigilant about giving the Spirit proper attention and due reverence. But it may just be the case that the person of the Trinity who actually gets the least attention is not the third person but the first. There must be at least ten times as many books written on the Holy Spirit as on God the Father. And there is not even a name for the doctrine of God the Father. We study the Son in Christology and the Spirit in pneumatology, but there is no corresponding name for studying the Father (Father-ology? Very recently some writers have begun using the word Paterology). He is often left in the background—a highly exalted background, to be sure! But it is true that in our thoughts about God, we often struggle with Father-forgetfulness.

In this chapter, we will consider God the Holy Spirit in relation to God the Father and will gain clarity about both of these persons of the Trinity by pondering them together. Just as we know to appropriate beginnings to the Father ("maker of heaven and earth," as the creed says), we have learned to appropriate completions to the Spirit ("to him belongs . . . the consummation," as Mastricht says). Between this origin and this conclusion comes everything. Examining the Holy Spirit in relation to the Father is an opportunity to think some very large thoughts about God and his ways. Our initial approach will be through the Old Testament.

Promise and Fulfillment

In the Old Testament, God promises to send forth his Spirit or, more precisely, to pour out his Spirit. The most famous of the prophetic promises is in the second chapter of Joel:

> And it shall come to pass afterward,
>   that I will pour out my Spirit on all flesh;
> your sons and your daughters shall prophesy,
>   your old men shall dream dreams,
>   and your young men shall see visions.
> Even on the male and female servants
>   in those days I will pour out my Spirit. (vv. 28–29)

"Pour out" is a striking and unexpected image. It is unexpected because what we normally pour out is some sort of liquid. The Spirit is not some kind of subpersonal liquid! But this biblical language communicates to us the magnitude and definiteness of this prophesied event. God will not sprinkle his Spirit around here and there, or operate secretly and unobserved by way of his Spirit, or in fact be subtle or ignorable on this great day; there will be a deluge of the Spirit of God.

The outpouring of the Spirit of God is a major event in God's plan for Israel and the world. In fact, in passage after passage of Scripture, this outpouring shows up as more than just the next big thing in a series of divine actions; it stands out as the final, culminating thing. The outpouring of the Spirit of God is eschatological, a blessing reserved for the end times. The other things that God does lead up to it and lean forward in anticipation of it, but the actual outpouring of God's Spirit is to occur "afterward," that is, as the final event. The prophecy of Joel is that in those last days, God will pour out his Spirit on all flesh, and all kinds of people (old and young, men and women) will have supernatural knowledge of God.

The promise is repeated by many prophets, with an overall similarity but minor shifts of emphasis. Isaiah says less about the variety of the people who will be transformed when the Spirit is poured out eschatologically and more about how it will be a blessing that renews the natural environment. Through a time of desolation, fields will be left unfruitful and cities will be abandoned "until the Spirit is poured upon us from on high, and the wilderness becomes a fruitful field, and the fruitful field is deemed a forest" (Isa. 32:15).

The prophecies of Ezekiel also feature the promised Spirit, making connections to the way the Spirit will renew the people of God and establish them as true covenant partners to God, obedient from within:

> I will give you a new heart, and a new spirit I will put within you. And I will remove the heart of stone from your flesh and give you a heart of flesh. And I will put my Spirit within you, and cause you to walk in my statutes and be careful to obey my rules. You shall dwell in the land that I gave to your fathers, and you shall be my people, and I will be your God. (Ezek. 36:26–28)

In a way that is typical of Ezekiel's message, this internal renewal of the covenant people will lead to a deeper knowledge of who God is. His identity as the Lord their God will be established because he will demonstrate himself to be the same one who brought them out of Egypt, sent them into exile, and then restored them to the promised land. All of this culminates in God making himself present to them in the outpouring of the Spirit:

> Then they shall know that I am the LORD their God, because I sent them into exile among the nations and then assembled them into their own land. I will leave none of them remaining among the nations anymore. And I will not hide my face anymore from them, when I pour out my Spirit upon the house of Israel, declares the Lord GOD. (Ezek. 39:28–29)

Of course Ezekiel's pneumatology also features the famous vision of the valley of dry bones (chapter 37), in which a mighty army rises up, animated by a wind from God that blows into their lungs to become their own breath.

To survey the full prophetic witness of the Old Testament about the promised outpouring of the Spirit is to see all God's ways converge: people unified, hearts renewed, laws obeyed, the land restored, and God made manifest! So many things will come to fulfillment when God pours out his Spirit on all flesh.

We have begun looking at this outpouring from the perspective of the Old Testament. There are some great advantages to starting with this prophetic vantage point.

First, anticipation. The promise-and-fulfillment approach helps us retrace, in our own understanding, the actual historical and developmental way God made himself known. Or, to put it canonically, it lets us start at the beginning of the Bible and read forward intelligently, with the result that we have a better-stocked understanding of what promises are being kept when we reach the New Testament. In the case of the Holy

Spirit, that means that when he emerges more obviously as a definite person with a distinct name, we can have the "aha" moment of recognition. He shows up in person with all the accumulated force of expectation, losing none of his massive power but gaining in clarity and definiteness. (This is part of what we called the always-already character of knowing the Holy Spirit, in chapter 1.)

Second, the Father. The prophetic approach highlights for us the relation between the Father and the Spirit. Although the sentence "the Father sends the Holy Spirit" is not an Old Testament way of talking, it is manifestly the real meaning of the prophetic message. We learn this more explicitly from the New Testament. For example, Jesus tells the disciples, "I am sending the promise of my Father upon you" (Luke 24:49), by which he means the Holy Spirit, "promise of my Father" being almost a name that Jesus uses to identify the Spirit here. Jesus instructs the disciples to "wait for the promise of the Father, which, he said, 'you heard from me'" (Acts 1:4). In light of this, we can look back and see that there was always a Father-Spirit dynamic at work in this promise. Even when God said in terse, oracular form, "I will pour out my Spirit," what was being voiced was God the Father's promise of the mission of God the Holy Spirit. Doctrinally speaking, "the Spirit of the LORD" means the third person of the Trinity, who proceeds from the first person of the Trinity. So, enriched by Trinitarian insight, we can reread the promises of the Old Testament as one massive testimony to the Spirit's relation to the Father. You may think you know very little about the relation between these two persons of the Trinity, but in fact you already know something big and important: the Father desires to pour out his Holy Spirit on all flesh.

Third, eschatology. We get to know the eschatological Holy Spirit as the one whom the Father promises to send in the last days, and then we meet him in person when he is poured out in fulfillment of the promise. This mainly happens on the day of Pentecost, reported in the book of Acts. The link between Joel 2 and Acts 2 is one of the clearest and most explicit fulfillment formulas in the entire Bible. When the Holy Spirit falls on the disciples in Jerusalem at Pentecost, Peter declares to the astonished crowd, "This is what was uttered through the prophet Joel," and then cites over a dozen lines of the prophecy from Joel. It is a clear case of a promise made and a promise kept. It might lead us to think that the eschatological Holy Spirit has arrived in all his fullness in such a way that he no longer belongs to the future work of God. We might, in this way of thinking, put the Spirit on the biblical timeline as having been poured out at a point in our past, without remainder. We might admit that there are important, ongoing results and recognize his permanent presence in the church, but essentially we would be thinking of the Spirit's outpouring as the kind of eschatology that was future from the point of view of the Old Testament but now past from our point of view. We think of messianic prophecies that way; after all, the Old Testament prophets looked forward to the time when the Messiah would come, but we now look back to the time when the Messiah came.

But thinking this way about the Spirit would be a mistake. There is something more thoroughly or abidingly eschatological about the outpouring of the Holy Spirit. He continues to be a promise for our own future. That is, his status as a promise seems to be still in effect, even in this time after Pentecost, under the new covenant. Even when Peter cites Joel 2 as being fulfilled in Acts 2, he is not claiming that all of Joel's prophecies have now taken place—all the signs and wonders in the sky, the restoration of Jerusalem, and the judgment of the nations in the full eschatological day of the Lord. Instead, he is specifically pointing out that the promised Holy Spirit has been poured out on young and old, men and women, such that they testify about Jesus the Messiah, and that now at last "everyone who calls on the name of the LORD shall be saved" (Joel 2:32; cf. Acts 2:21).[1] In other words, the eschatological Spirit is in fact poured out at Pentecost, but that outpouring is only the beginning of "the last days."[2] He, the Holy Spirit, continues to have a future day that will be of even greater extent. Approaching pneumatology from the Old Testament marks the Spirit as abidingly eschatological.

We can also see the still-outstanding eschatological character of the Holy Spirit in the way the New Testament talks about him. God has "put his seal on us and given us his Spirit in our hearts as a guarantee" (2 Cor. 1:22; see also 2 Cor. 5:5). This word "guarantee" has the sense of a down payment (or "earnest money" in old-fashioned language). The idea is a financial pledge that genuinely secures as our present possession something that is in itself more of a future reality. In Ephesians Paul says that believers have been "sealed with the promised Holy Spirit, who is the guarantee of our inheritance until we acquire possession of it" (1:13–14). We could emphasize the future element even more by translating this very literally, "the Holy Spirit of promise, who is the down payment." That is, there are practically two hidden titles of the Spirit here: Spirit of promise and Spirit of down payment. Both underline his eschatological character. Old-covenant believers looked forward to an end-times outpouring of the Holy Spirit of promise; new-covenant

---

1. While the big events are clear enough, there is a great deal going on in the New Testament fulfillment of Joel 2. See Daniel J. Treier, "The Fulfillment of Joel 2:28–32: A Multiple-Lens Approach," *Journal of the Evangelical Theological Society* 40 (March 1997): 13–26.

2. Where Joel's prophecy only says "afterward," Peter's interpretive quotation of it specifies "in the last days." For details and a full discussion, see I. Howard Marshall, "Acts," in *Commentary on the New Testament Use of the Old Testament*, ed. D. A. Carson and G. K. Beale (Grand Rapids, MI: Baker Academic, 2007), 534.

believers are indwelt by the Holy Spirit of promise, who has touched down here but whose wingspan extends beyond us into our final future as well. The third person of the Trinity is the Spirit of the last days, and in Scripture, "the last days" have a near edge and a far edge.

All this biblical theology of the eschatological outpouring of the Holy Spirit fits snugly into our Trinitarian theological structure. It makes sense that the person of the Trinity who proceeds from the Father in all eternity would be the one who is poured out on all flesh in salvation history. Rehearsing the Trinitarian sequence that runs "from the Father, through the Son, in the Holy Spirit," we can see how deeply fitting it is that all of God's ways tend toward, and terminate in, the work of the Holy Spirit. Recalling that (while every external operation of the Trinity is inseparably united) we appropriate beginnings to the Father and conclusions to the Holy Spirit, we are not surprised to find eschatology as the special province in which the Spirit of promise shows his particular character.

Big-Picture Pneumatology

Once we come to understand the Father's promise of the Holy Spirit, a stunningly large vista of salvation history opens up in front of us. Think of it this way: God the Father's plan has always been to dwell among his people, and the Holy Spirit is, in person, the fulfillment of that plan.

Over and over in his covenant promises to Israel, God connects the reciprocal formula "I will be your God, and you shall be my people" with the goal of living in the midst of his people. "I will dwell among the people of Israel and will be their God," he says, explaining that the very goal of the exodus itself was God making himself known and dwelling in their midst: "And they shall know that I am the LORD their God, who brought them out of the land of Egypt that I might dwell among them. I am the LORD their God" (Exod. 29:45–46). Many of the laws of Leviticus have to do with making the camp of Israel a place in which God and the people can live in close proximity, with the result that "I will make my dwelling among you, and my soul shall not abhor you. And I will walk among you and will be your God, and you shall be my people" (Lev. 26:11–12). Both of these passages are picked up by Paul in encouraging Christians to be holy: "What agreement has the temple of God with idols? For we are the temple of the living God; as God said, 'I will make my dwelling among them and walk among them, and I will be their God, and they shall be my people'" (2 Cor. 6:16). And at the end of Revelation, John hears a loud voice from God's throne saying, "Behold, the dwelling place of God is with man. He will dwell with them, and they will be his people, and God himself will be with them as their God" (Rev. 21:3). If we reached back to the divine-human fellowship in the garden of Eden, we would have a Bible-spanning, Genesis-to-Revelation theology of God dwelling with, and even more radically in, humanity.

Indeed, this divine plan for indwelling is grounded in a desire that runs so deep in the heart of God that it reaches back further than the purposes of redemption. It goes all the way back into the purposes of creation itself, for why there are creatures at all—for God to be among. To put it another way, if God intends to dwell among humans, he first has to make humans. So his first step would be to create them, in order to then take step two and live among them. And in order for there to be humans, there has to be a whole created world for them to be in. So God's plan for dwelling in people is not only "older than dirt," but it's the reason there is dirt. If divine indwelling is the goal, then creation itself is a means to that goal.

This is an intentionally expansive way of putting the implications of the Father's promise to pour out the Holy Spirit. But putting things in this maximal way raises three issues that need to be clarified.

First, when we say God desired to dwell among us, we need to be careful never to describe this as the kind of desire that comes from any lack, deficit, or neediness on his part. Remember that God in himself has never had any unmet needs. We have already seen that the very idea of God having his own fully divine Spirit means that he does not exist in the middle of some extrinsic atmosphere or environment that he draws his life from; he is all he needs. God will never say to a creature, "You complete me," no matter how much he loves that creature. Love that is divine does not work that way, since love that is divine is already complete. The triune God, though absolutely one, is not personally solitary. We can see this most obviously by considering the eternal fellowship of Father, Son, and Holy Spirit, in which there is no empty space for loneliness or isolation. To put it as positively as possible, God is blessed eternally sufficient to himself, delighting in the love and light that make the divine life. Once we have reminded ourselves of this deep truth of God's eternal fullness of glory, we can safely go on and say what God wants, chooses, sets his good pleasure on, desires to bring about, or freely elects to do.[3] God desires to dwell in the midst of his people, not out of need or greed but freely, truly, and deeply. The more clearly we understand that God does not need us, the more clearly we can rejoice that he wants to live among us by the Spirit.

Second, when we say that God desired to dwell among us and then did so, we have skipped a step. Notice the sequence.

---

3. See Steven J. Duby, *God in Himself: Scripture, Metaphysics, and the Task of Christian Theology* (Downers Grove, IL: IVP Academic, 2019).

First, God intended to dwell among us; second, he promised to dwell among us; and third, he poured out his Holy Spirit to dwell among us. It makes for a smooth story, but in telling it we have failed to mention the major obstacle to divine indwelling that the Bible brings up, which is the problem of sin. There is a fundamental opposition between holiness and sin such that a holy God will not simply dwell among or in an unholy people. As he works out his purpose and plan, God decisively overcomes this obstacle by means of atonement. Ultimately, he atones for the sins of his people and sets them apart (that is, sanctifies them) to be his own. In fact, the biblical and historical outworking of the atonement involves its own fascinating story with its own prophetic foretelling, typological unfolding, and final accomplishment. In order to atone for sin and make it possible for God to dwell among humans, the Son of God took human nature to himself and accomplished salvation in that human nature.

Taking this into account, we can retell the story of divine indwelling in a fuller way. God desired to dwell among us, but the obstacle of sin intervened. To achieve his final goal, God the Father sent God the Son to atone for sin, which prepared the way for God the Holy Spirit to be poured out on all flesh. The temple of humanity needed to be cleansed in order for God to dwell in it. In the atonement, the Son of God took on the temple of human nature and cleansed it in his own person. On that basis, the Holy Spirit was then poured out onto reconciled humanity. We temporarily omitted the step of atonement only in order to highlight the big picture so that we could reintroduce atonement as a kind of means to the desired end: God in us by the Spirit.

Third, in temporarily skipping the subject of the atonement, we also temporarily set aside the central role of the Son of God.

It is high time we brought him back into focus because none of God's ways make sense until we understand them as being centered on Jesus Christ. And even though the next chapter will be devoted directly to considering the Son in relation to the Spirit, to omit him even from this chapter on the Father would involve a serious distortion of what we are saying now. So, then, what does the Son have to do with the indwelling of God? Much in every way. He is the one, as we have just seen, who accomplishes the work that makes that indwelling possible. He does this, moreover, by being the one human being in whom the Holy Spirit dwells fully and the one who dispenses the Spirit without measure (John 3:34). When we think of the Son and his work from the vantage point of the Father's plan to pour out the Holy Spirit, we can see the Son as the one who accomplishes the Spirit's indwelling first and foundationally in his own personal human nature. Let us say this with as much Christological precision as possible: the Son's hypostatic union is the basis for human nature's reception of the Holy Spirit. And let us say it with as much Trinitarian precision as possible: divine indwelling in humanity is an undivided work of the entire Trinity, carried out from the Father, through the Son, in the Holy Spirit. It is from the Father who pours out, through the Son's accomplished atonement, the Holy Spirit's personal presence in believers.

When we think about this from the point of view of the Father pouring out the Spirit, the work of the Son functions as a sort of means to an end. We are not used to thinking of the Son that way because the Bible rightly teaches us to focus our attention on Christ as the center of God's ways. Also, the Holy Spirit himself is in the business of showing us the things that belong to the Son (John 16:14). But for the sake of understanding the full scope of pneumatology, it is helpful to train our eyes momentarily on the indwelling of the Holy Spirit as the goal and culmination of the Father's plan. First is the atonement and then, on its foundation, the indwelling. In that sense, the atonement made by Jesus Christ is God's appointed means to his chosen end, which is indwelling by the Spirit. God with us, Emmanuel, did his great work among us to set the stage for God in us by the Spirit. Sin was an obstacle in the path, which the death of Christ removed.

Of course, from another point of view—the Christological point of view—the Father's plan to dwell with his people was perfectly accomplished in the incarnation of his Son. By taking on human nature, the Son crossed the great divide between Creator and creature; by atoning for our sin, he healed the rift between holy and unholy; by then taking his seat at the Father's right hand, he brought human nature itself into God's presence. In relation to all this, the work of the Holy Spirit is a matter of taking that redemption completed in Christ and applying it personally to believers. From this point of view, the work of the Spirit seems to be almost an adjunct or extension of the work of the Son. The Spirit's work may be absolutely necessary, but what it is necessary for is to take the work of the Son and distribute it. The outpoured Spirit mediates the presence of the incarnate one during the time between his ascension and his return. If we describe these matters sloppily, we risk setting up the Son and the Holy Spirit in some sort of contention over whose work is in service to whose. They are in no such competition! Their missions are perfectly ordered toward each other, and perfectly coordinated. Neither mission would be itself without the other.

Everything about our salvation is done in an inseparable operation that comes from the Father, through the Son, and in the Spirit. But when we consider this unified work from the perspective of the Holy Spirit's relation to the Father, what comes forward for our attention is the way the Son's work prepares the ground for the outpouring of the Holy Spirit. On the other hand, when we consider this unified work from the perspective of the Holy Spirit's relation to the Son, what comes forward for our attention is the way the Spirit applies and extends what the Son perfectly accomplishes. These truths are complementary. They demand each other. We have to split them up into separate chapters just to let our attention have enough time to take them both in turn.

Big-picture pneumatology has its foundation in the Father's intention to pour out his Spirit on all flesh. We should never pretend that big-picture pneumatology makes sense without its necessary connection to Christology and atonement (that is, the person and work of the Son). But we need to turn our eyes to it often enough to refresh our awareness of the Holy Spirit. By temporarily focusing our attention on the Father-Spirit relation, we are able to see more clearly a vital aspect of the Bible's message. The Father-Spirit relation imparts a certain universal scope to pneumatology.

Of the many new vistas that open up for us to contemplate along the Father-Spirit line, we should, at least in passing, mention world missions. The Father's desire to pour out his Spirit on all flesh makes God's plan for all nations around the world more evident. The message of Scripture pulsates with God's desire to be known deeply by all nations and to pour out his Spirit on all flesh. When we think of world evangelism, our minds often go directly to the Great Commission given by the risen Jesus (Matt. 28:18–20). But it could also go to Pentecost (Acts 2), when the Spirit ("the promise" from the Father) brought the power to obey the commission. Big-picture pneumatology includes this vast horizon of the global spread of

God's good news to all people. The Father is seeking people to worship him in Spirit and in truth (John 4:23). True worship of the Father necessarily takes place in the outpoured Spirit.

Worship in the Spirit

We have seen that the Father desires to pour out his Spirit, that he promises to do so, and that on that basis he sends the Spirit. And we have glanced at the fact that the final result of this outpouring is the Spirit's indwelling, God by the Spirit taking up residence in believers. Now it is time to say explicitly what the result of that indwelling will be. It will be worship. True worship is always worship empowered by the personal presence of the Holy Spirit, creating the atmosphere in which it is possible for creatures to worship God. Just as all divine action comes from the Father, through the Son, and in the Holy Spirit, so all human participation in that action begins in the Spirit, goes through the Son, and returns to the Father. We can take that helpful set of prepositions, *from-through-in*, and run it in reverse in the form *in-through-to*. The shape of God's action toward us is perfectly mirrored in our movement toward God, since our movement toward God can only happen in response to that prior divine action. When we worship the Father in the power of the Holy Spirit, we complete the entire cycle that runs outward from the Father (through the Son in the Spirit) and brings us back to the Father (through the Son in the Spirit).

In Ephesians Paul describes the Christian community as coming together in precisely this way when Christ creates peace: ". . . for through him we both have access in one Spirit to the Father" (Eph. 2:18). The dynamic of reconciliation that we see here (through the Son, in the Spirit, to the Father) is the same basic grammar governing all movement toward God. In the immediate context of Ephesians 2, Paul is referring to the unity of Gentiles with Jews, as "both have access" to the Father and are brought together in his presence. Paul draws out the implications for a Christian unity that spans ethnic and cultural differences, breaking down walls and killing hostility (2:13–16). But this *in-through-to* dynamic follows directly from the *from-through-in* dynamic at work in the first half of Ephesians 2, where believers are made alive together with Christ and saved by grace through faith. We might draw it out more explicitly by saying that in the first half of Ephesians 2, salvation comes from the Father ("God, being rich in mercy, because of the great love with which he loved us," 2:4), through the Son ("he made us alive together with Christ . . . and raised us up with him," 2:5–6), in the Spirit (who is left unmentioned in this passage, but who is active in both raising Christ and uniting us to his resurrection, Rom. 8:11). All this sets the stage for worship; "access" means coming into God's presence appropriately, that is, in the one Holy Spirit.

John Owen calls this passage, Ephesians 2:18, a "heavenly directory" that lays out the full scope of communion with the triune God. Within the scope of God's oneness, the ordered relation of the persons is evident: "Here is a distinction of the persons, as to their operations, but not at all as to their being the object of our worship."[4] Owen is eager to remind us that the Holy Spirit, having the divine nature, is himself the object of proper worship. In fact, Owen provides solid arguments for the fact that rightly worshiping any of the persons of the Trinity involves worshiping all three as the one God: "It is impossible to worship any one person, and not worship the whole Trinity."[5]

---

4. John Owen, *Communion with the Triune God*, ed. Kelly M. Kapic and Justin Taylor (Wheaton, IL: Crossway, 2007), 420. See also Ryan M. McGraw, *A Heavenly Directory: Trinitarian Piety, Public Worship, and a Reassessment of John Owen's Theology* (Göttingen, Germany: Vandenhoeck & Ruprecht, 2014).

5. Owen, *Communion with the Triune God*, 419–20.

But to grasp the distinct importance of the Spirit in worship, we need to focus on the fact that he is the person in whom all grace-enabled approaches to God take place. The key is that little preposition *in*. Remember that the divine life of the Trinity itself is an inseparable life from the Father, through the Son, in the Holy Spirit. And the indivisible work of the Trinity toward us likewise takes place from the Father, through the Son, in the Holy Spirit. In making his point about worship, Owen rehearses all this and takes us on to the next step: "Not only in the *emanation* of grace from God, and the *illapses* of the Spirit on us, but also in all our approaches unto God, is the same distinction observed."[6]

This may seem like a lot of heavy Trinitarian equipment to bring to the task of explaining the work of the Holy Spirit in worship, but Owen rightly sees it as necessary. We have to have a sense of who the Spirit is in himself and in relation to the Father in the first place, before we can appreciate who he is toward us and in relation to our worship in the second place. So Owen unpacks the *from-through-in* formula a bit more by putting it in terms of how God reaches down to us with grace: "The Father does it by the way of original authority; the Son by the way of communicating from a purchased treasury; the Holy Spirit by the way of immediate efficacy."[7] It is the "immediate efficacy" that captures the sense of being in the Spirit in worship. In communion with the triune God, the Holy Spirit is our indwelling place of contact.

No wonder, then, that Paul exhorts us later in Ephesians to be "praying at all times in the Spirit, with all prayer and supplication" (6:18). In a booklength meditation on this verse, Puritan theologian Nathaniel Vincent (1639–1697) noted that

6. Owen, *Communion with the Triune God*, 96; emphasis original.
7. Owen, *Communion with the Triune God*, 104.

the phrase "in the Spirit" actually "refers both to the Spirit of him that prays, and also to the Spirit of God, who helps to pray."[8] All kinds of prayer and supplication are to be offered spiritually in both senses: from our spiritual nature and in the Holy Spirit of God. Vincent links the Spirit's work in prayer to the work of Christ, arguing that the Holy Spirit "directs believers unto Christ, as the alone prevailing Advocate."[9] But it is the Spirit himself who does that directing, as the one in whom prayer takes place.

John Owen gives further detail on the Spirit's work in prayer. Picking up on God's promise to "pour out . . . the spirit of grace and of supplications" (Zech. 12:10 KJV), Owen argues that the Holy Spirit works in us in two ways: by "giving *gracious inclinations* and dispositions in us unto this duty" of prayer and "by giving a gracious *ability* for the discharge of it in a due manner."[10] That is, the Holy Spirit makes us want to pray and then gives us the power to pray. The first step, making us want to pray, is foundational because something in our fallen nature is habitually resistant to approaching God in prayer: "Of ourselves, naturally, we are averse from any converse and intercourse with God, as being alienated from living unto him, by the ignorance and vanity of our minds." It takes the animating work of the Holy Spirit to stir us up and move us toward God. It is the Holy Spirit "who prepareth, disposeth, and inclineth the hearts of believers unto the exercise" of prayer "with delight and spiritual complacency. And where this is not, no prayer is acceptable unto God. He delights not in those cries which an unwilling mind is pressed and forced unto by earthly

---

8. Nathanael Vincent, *The Spirit of Prayer* (London: Thomas Parkhurst, 1677), 69.

9. Vincent, *Spirit of Prayer,* 74. Vincent immediately cites Eph. 2:18.

10. John Owen, *A Discourse of the Work of the Holy Spirit in Prayer,* vol. 4, *Works of John Owen*, ed. Thomas Russell (London: Richard Baynes, 1826), 40; emphasis original.

desires, distress, or misery."[11] When we pray willingly, from a heart inclined to seek God and drawn by an inward desire to commune with him, we see once more that both meanings of "pray in the Spirit" are operative. In the Holy Spirit of God, we pray spiritually rather than merely externally or by compulsion.

In a second step, the Spirit also gives us a "gracious ability" to pray rightly. This is because the fulfillment of Zechariah's promise of an outpoured "spirit of grace and of supplications" can become a matter of our actual experience. The experience is described by Paul: "The Spirit helps us in our weakness. For we do not know what to pray for as we ought, but the Spirit himself intercedes for us with groanings too deep for words" (Rom. 8:26). Owen concludes that the Holy Spirit is truly a Spirit of supplication "as he communicates a gift or ability unto persons to exercise all his graces in the way and duty of prayer. This is that which he is here promised for, and promised to be poured out for; that is, to be given in an abundant and plentiful manner. Wherever he is bestowed in the accomplishment of this promise, he both disposeth the hearts of men to pray, and enableth them so to do."[12] The Father, who seeks worshipers in Spirit and in truth, sends forth the Spirit in whom the worship can be true:

> To come to God as a Father, through Christ, by the help and assistance of the Holy Spirit, revealing him as a Father unto us, and enabling us to go to him as a Father, how full of sweetness and satisfaction is it! Without a due apprehension of God in this relation, no man can pray as he ought. And hereof we have no sense, herewith we have no acquaintance, but by the Holy Ghost.[13]

11. Owen, *Work of the Spirit in Prayer*, 43.
12. Owen, *Work of the Spirit in Prayer*, 42.
13. Owen, *Work of the Spirit in Prayer*, 82.

Deep Calls to Deep

What does it mean that the Spirit, in helping us pray, "intercedes for us with groanings too deep for words" (Rom. 8:26)? It would be misleading to think of this as a statement about the Holy Spirit being animated by his own painful groanings, as if he were somehow racked by longing and suffering from a lack of fulfillment. There have, in fact, been interpreters who took the expression to indicate this, but many of those interpreters, to be consistent in their views, had to go ahead and consider the Spirit as something less than divine. Subordinating him to a nondivine status, these non-Trinitarian interpreters would even consider him to be engaged in prayer himself, a creature praying to the Creator. But the Spirit is God. Romans 8:26, in other words, is not about the Holy Spirit being a creature who groans and prays to God alongside us. Instead, it is about God drawing so close to us that he supports and empowers our prayers at a deeper level than we can even articulate. Indeed the Holy Spirit is closer to us than we are to ourselves, because while parts of our inner life may be inaccessible even to our own minds, none of them are closed off to the Holy Spirit. The Spirit "intercedes for the saints according to the will of God" (Rom. 8:27), not with his own inarticulate groanings (for he is neither inarticulate nor suffering) but with ours. In his power and fullness, he empowers and fills our groanings. If you hear deep, spiritual groaning in prayer, it is from your spirit and also from God's, but in different ways.

John Owen explores this dynamic in another context that is helpful for comparison. Romans 8 also tells us that believers "have received the Spirit of adoption as sons, by whom we cry, 'Abba! Father!'" (Rom. 8:15). Notice who cries "Abba"—we do, by the Spirit. But when Paul returns to this same teaching in Galatians 4, he says it differently: "God has sent the

Spirit of his Son into our hearts, crying, 'Abba! Father!'" (Gal. 4:6). Notice who cries "Abba"—the Spirit does, from within our hearts. "His acting in us, and our acting by him, is expressed by the same word. And the inquiry here is, how in the same duty he is said to cry in us, and we are said to cry in him." [14] The cry belongs to both, but "in diverse respects," says Owen. "As it is an act of grace and spiritual power, it is his, or it is wrought in us by him alone. As it is a duty performed by us, by virtue of his assistance, it is ours; by him we cry Abba Father." [15] There is a two-sidedness to the Spirit's work in prayer, divine from one side and human from the other. Often when we come upon a human-divine duality in Christian theology, we think of explaining it Christologically, with reference to the incarnation of the Son of God in human nature. But here we are trying to think pneumatologically, not reckoning with the incarnation. The Spirit after all is not incarnate, but indwelling.

That indwelling is, in fact, the key. It is the Spirit's interiority or depth within the believer that gives his work its human side. When the Father sends his Spirit into us, the cry "Abba" sounds forth from our innermost depths as a human word spoken from our deepest hearts and simultaneously as the same word from the heart of God. [16] That is how deeply the Holy Spirit dwells within the redeemed. And this takes on more significance when we remember what we said in chapter 2 about the Holy Spirit being in God. The one who is in God by his eternal nature is

14. Owen, *Work of the Spirit in Prayer*, 52.
15. Owen, *Work of the Spirit in Prayer*, 52.
16. "Abba" might be what we would expect the Son, not the Spirit, to cry to the Father. The Father is not, after all, Father of the Spirit, but of the Son. There is a lot happening here! It is an instance of the Spirit doing what Jesus said he would do: "He will take what is mine and declare it to you" (John 16:14). And both times he mentions this ministry, Paul distinctly identifies the Spirit as "the Spirit of adoption" (Rom. 8:15) and "the Spirit of his Son" (Gal. 4:6). So the Spirit speaks and enables Son language while being fully himself rather than the Son.

also in us by grace. When we start using this "deep within" language about the Holy Spirit, we have to reckon with him being both deep within God and also deep within creatures. He indwells the Father and the children. The Father pours out his Spirit on flesh and seeks those who will worship him in Spirit and truth.

We have been led to see this double depth of the Holy Spirit by considering his ministry of prayer and worship. But his double depth has a very wide significance for understanding how the Bible talks about the Holy Spirit (that is, how the Holy Spirit talks about himself). Because he is simultaneously in the heart of God and in the heart of believers, Scripture routinely transfers to him certain attributes that are either properly human or in some way arise at the very point where the human encounter with the divine happens. We have already seen the way "Abba" is a human cry spoken by the indwelling Spirit and how the groaning proper to creaturely neediness is also nested under the Spirit's superintendence and made his own, as it were.[17] Similarly, the Holy Spirit can be grieved, as Ephesians warns us: "Do not grieve the Holy Spirit of God, by whom you were sealed for the day of redemption" (Eph. 4:30). The Holy Spirit is not more *grievable* than the Father, considered either according to his divine nature or his personal distinction. In the strictly theological sense, of course, the Spirit is not properly grievable at all, since he is the impassible God and cannot be subjected to suffering.[18] But the Spirit dwells in double depth, at

---

17. Gordon Fee, *God's Empowering Presence: The Holy Spirit in the Letters of Paul* (Peabody, MA: Hendrickson, 1994), 582.

18. Lancelot Andrewes captures the sense of the verse in a sermon on it: "We may, on our parts, 'grieve,' that is, do what in us lieth to 'grieve' Him," since "if it were possible by any means in the world that that grief could be made to fall into the divine essence," we would make it happen. But owing to "the high supereminent perfection of His nature that is not capable of it," the Spirit is not in fact harmed. Lancelot Andrewes, *Ninety-Six Sermons* (Oxford, UK: John Henry Parker, 1841), 3:206; from a sermon delivered in 1613. Grieving the Spirit is like robbing God of his glory: attempted robbery, utterly real on our side, but not inflicting any loss of glory on God.

the interior frontier between God's holiness and humanity's sin. When we recall that this line from Ephesians 4 is Paul's application of the Old Testament warning that the redeemed people of God "rebelled and grieved his Holy Spirit" (Isa. 63:10), we begin to see the broader pattern.

The Bible often gives prominence to the Holy Spirit precisely when it indicates the point of conflict between divine and human. E. H. Bickersteth, reflecting on this phenomenon, stated it as a principle: "It is the peculiar office of the Holy Spirit to strive with men."[19] If this is correct, it helps explain why the Holy Spirit, who does not become incarnate, nevertheless strives, groans, cries out, and can be grieved. It is not to be explained by anything about his eternal nature or his personal distinction within the Trinity but by his office of double depth. He is the one who is by nature in the Father and by grace indwells us.

Indeed, as we try to understand the way God draws near to us and abides with us spiritually, there is something especially helpful in focusing on the Father-Spirit relation. The Son, as the actually incarnate person of the Trinity, is almost too obviously linked to human realities. We are in danger of answering all our theological questions prematurely with the single answer, "Because of the incarnation." But the incarnation answer does not apply directly and personally to the Father or the Holy Spirit. By following Scripture's guidance about the double depth of the Holy Spirit in God and the faithful, we gain a better understanding of God's ways with humanity and an insight into the Holy Spirit in person.

19. E. H. Bickersteth, *The Spirit of Life: or, Scripture Testimony to the Divine Person and Work of the Holy Ghost* (London: Religious Tract Society, n.d.), 67. Further instances of the Spirit striving with humans, including fallen humanity, may be found in Gen. 6:3, Gal. 5:17, and James 4:5, though the interpretation of these passages is difficult. The last two in particular are so obscure that it would be unwise to base any significant doctrinal conclusions on them alone.

The Spirit Proceeds from the Father

We should conclude this chapter on the Father and the Holy Spirit by making one brief statement about the third person's eternal relation of origin from the first. We have traced the Father-Spirit relation across the Old Testament and into the New, from the depths of God to the depths of the human heart. But these are only the outskirts of his ways, the outer works of the Father in the Holy Spirit *toward us*. What can we say about the eternal identity of the Holy Spirit in relation to the Father in the Trinity itself? What do we learn by directing our attention to the Father-Spirit relation in the eternal, triune life?

The question matters because the Father and the Holy Spirit would have stood in an eternal relation to each other even if we had never existed. If the Spirit had never "hover[ed] over the face of the waters" (Gen. 1:2) to form and fill the cosmos, he would nevertheless always already have been fully alive within the being of God, one of the Trinity, Spirit of the Father and of the Son. In this chapter we have traced the Spirit coming from the Father to us; this is his coming forth, his being sent outward, his mission. But behind that mission is the eternal procession. Remember that *mission*, in Trinitarian theology, is a special word for the way a person of the Trinity is present to us creatures on the basis of an eternal procession within God. That eternal procession itself is what we need to say something about now.

When Jesus taught his disciples about the Holy Spirit, he told them they would be empowered "when the Helper comes, whom I will send to you from the Father, the Spirit of truth, who proceeds from the Father" (John 15:26). Notice the sending and the proceeding. First he describes the mission ("I will send"), and then he describes something deeper than the mission: ". . . who proceeds from the Father." Jesus goes out of his way to underline where the Spirit is from, and that fromness has two levels: sent from and proceeding from.

The word "proceeds" occurs only once in the New Testament, here in John 15:26. Theologians have recognized its special status as a guide to discerning the Spirit's eternal fromness.[20] Gregory of Nazianzus appealed to it directly as a term introduced by a truly superior theologian, that is, Jesus himself.[21] To say that the Spirit proceeds from the Father is to locate him within the being of God, recognizing him as above every creature (since creatures come forth from the entire inseparable, triune God). It also picks him out as being a distinct person from the Son, since proceeding is not the same as being begotten. When Jesus tells us that the Holy Spirit "proceeds from the Father," he is revealing a great deal about the Spirit's distinct identity. The Nicene Creed picked up this exact phrase in its statement about the Holy Spirit, calling him "Lord and giver of life, who proceeds from the Father, who with the Father and the Son together is worshipped and glorified." Saying that he is "worshipped and glorified" together "with the Father and the Son" is to ensconce him fully within deity along with the other persons of the Trinity, while using the John 15:26 phrase, "he proceeds from the Father," points out the Spirit's personal (hypostatic) distinctness.

20. In Protestant theology, the Leiden Synopsis says that procession "is ascribed in the sacred writings uniquely to the Holy Spirit, as his personal characteristic property," and that "all the ancient interpreters understand the well-known passage [John 15:26] . . . as being about the eternal procession of the Holy Spirit." Leiden Synopsis, Disputation 9, par. 11–12, in *Synopsis Purioris Theologiae / Synopsis of a Purer Theology: Latin Text and English Translation*, ed. Dolf te Velde (Leiden, Netherlands: Brill, 2014), 1:235–37.

21. Gregory of Nazianzus, "Oration 31:8," in *On God and Christ: The Five Theological Orations and Two Letters to Cledonius* (Crestwood, NY: St. Vladimir's Seminary Press, 2002), 122.

The Holy Spirit, within the divine life, comes forth from the Father in a particular way, and that way is distinct from the Son's. As the church fathers often pointed out, if the second and third persons came from the first person in the same exact way, they would be two Sons of the Father. So when speaking of the Holy Spirit, they gave special honor to the fact of his procession. Even if they gladly admitted they could not declare the exact nature of the Spirit's procession (any more than they could declare the exact nature of the Son's begetting), they insisted that this was enough, to know that Son and Spirit come from the Father in different ways.

In geometry there is a custom of marking lines as congruent or noncongruent with the simple symbols called "hatch marks." Consider figure 3.1:

Figure 3.1

Geometers can know that the line on the left (one hatch mark) is not the same as the line on the right (two hatch marks), even without being able to say anything more positive about what the lines are. Some Trinitarian knowledge is like that. Because it is based strictly on revelation, it sometimes leaves us in the position of having to accept what has been made known, even when we are not able to peek behind the curtain to see why these things are as they are. "We have been taught that there is a difference between generation and procession," says John of Damascus (675–749), "but what the manner of the difference is we have in no way been informed."[22] For our knowledge of the Holy Spirit, knowing that he proceeds from the Father (double hatch mark; not begotten), is already, as we have seen, knowing a great deal.

There is, however, a guiding image given to us by Scripture that can help us say a little bit more about the Holy Spirit's relation to the Father. We can say that it is breath-like. The Spirit is a depth of life in God the Father that comes forth from him in effective power. Basil of Caesarea (330–379) argued that this breathiness of the Holy Spirit enables us to say that he is neither a creature nor the Son: "The Spirit is described to be of God, not in the sense that all things are of God, but because He proceeds from the mouth of the Father, and is not begotten like the Son."[23] Breath, of course, has to be understood appropriately, in a way that is suitable to God. For Basil, "the comparison of the Spirit with breath does not mean that he is the same as human breath, which quickly dissipates upon exhalation, for the Spirit is a living being with the power of God to sanctify others."[24] So in addition to saying that the Son and the Spirit come from the Father differently, we can say that the Son is begotten or generated, while the Spirit is breathed or spirated.

The Holy Spirit proceeds from the Father. The Western theological tradition, especially since Augustine, has been eager to add "and also from the Son." In the next chapter we will turn our full attention to the relation between the Spirit and the Son and see the cogency of the Western expansion. But it is worth noting the unanimity of East and West on the broader doctrine that the Holy Spirit proceeds from the Father. We cannot

22. John of Damascus, *On the Orthodox Faith* (Crestwood, NY: St. Vladimir's Seminary Press, 2022), 78.

23. Basil the Great, *On the Holy Spirit* (Crestwood, NY: St. Vladimir's Seminary Press, 2001), 73.

24. Michael Haykin, "'The Lord, The Life-Giver': Confessing the Holy Spirit in the Fourth Century," *Journal of the Evangelical Theological Society* 62 (March 2019): 77.

afford to shrug off this point of agreement while rushing on to disagreements. In fact, even in the midst of disagreement, the Western tradition has gladly admitted that there is something special and unique about the way the Spirit proceeds from the Father; something about the Father-Spirit relation that uniquely anchors the Spirit's identity. Augustine himself (who is not just anybody in matters like this) said, "The Father is called the one from whom the Word is born and from whom the Holy Spirit principally proceeds." What is that little word "principally" doing there? Augustine tells us: "I added 'principally,' because we have found that the Holy Spirit also proceeds from the Son. But this too was given to the Son by the Father."[25]

The Eastern tradition has jealously guarded the special word "proceeds" (John 15:26), recognizing in it a precious truth about the Spirit's unique relation to the Father. But the West can also join in and confess that the Spirit proceeds from the Father *principally*. In this chapter we have paid close attention to the Father-Spirit relation and seen how it rewards us with important insights into the Bible's presentation of the Holy Spirit: the promise of the Father, the Spirit of supplications, the indweller who is in the depths of God and the depths of humanity.

To make these Father-Spirit truths more prominent, we had to temporarily avoid speaking very much about the Son. But it is high time we reintroduced him, because there can be no Sonless pneumatology, and he stands at the center of all things.

---

25. Augustine, *The Trinity*, trans. Edmund Hill (New York: New City Press, 1991), 419. The Latin word Augustine uses here is just *principaliter*.

4

The Holy Spirit and the Son

There is such a close connection between the Son and the Holy Spirit that we sometimes all but lose one of them in the glory of the other. This strong connection is what we would expect, based on our Trinitarian theology, with its layers of unity: one God, the same divine essence, inseparable Trinitarian operations, and a single economy of salvation in which the Father sends forth both the Son and the Spirit (Gal. 4:4–6). But the same Trinitarian theology also teaches us that these persons are not each other. They can never be separated, but they can be distinguished, and they show their distinct personhood precisely in their relation to each other. Putting it paradoxically, you never get one without the other, which is how you can tell they are different. To discern the Holy Spirit more clearly, then, we must pay very close attention to the Son, especially in his incarnate ministry.

Their Trinitarian profiles become clearer as the biblical history unfolds. William Burt Pope (1822–1903) pointed out that "the Three Divine Persons are more or less revealed in the ancient economy; but their offices are not clearly and fully distinguished until the last days. The Son and the Spirit were alike in the Old Testament the promise; and are alike in the New sent as fulfilment of the promise."[1] When the time comes for their temporal missions, their distinction comes into sharper relief. We could say they are as clearly different as the incarnation and Pentecost, since the Son assumes human nature and the Holy Spirit is poured out on all flesh. This is true. Yet it might suggest a kind of relay race or tag team: first the Son arrives, and then later the Holy Spirit arrives. In fact, though, we should start noticing the Holy Spirit's work long before he makes his grand entrance at Pentecost. The Holy Spirit is always already present and active in the work of the incarnate Son.

The Holy Spirit in the Life of Jesus

From one perspective, as we saw in the previous chapter, the work of Jesus Christ prepared the way for the work of the Holy Spirit (atonement making indwelling possible). But if we view their closely integrated work from another point of view, we have to recognize the opposite truth as well: the work of the Holy Spirit prepared the way for the work of the incarnate Son. In fact, the very work that the Son did to prepare for the Spirit's indwelling was itself work that the Son did in the power of the Holy Spirit, by the enabling of the Holy Spirit, or in some other way in connection with the Holy Spirit. This truth is quite evident in the New Testament, and we only need to begin paying attention to it anywhere along the way to begin noticing that it is pervasive. Reading the life of Jesus while watching for signs of the Holy Spirit's activity is in fact one of the easiest and most rewarding exercises in all of theology. There is enormous

1. William Burt Pope, *A Higher Catechism of Theology* (London: T. Woolmer, 1883), 196–97. In the margin, Pope cites Gal. 4:4–6, Acts 2:33, and Acts 13:33.

pneumatological payoff from watching Jesus and considering the Holy Spirit.

To begin at the beginning of the Son's incarnate ministry, the Holy Spirit was directly operative with the conception and birth of Jesus. Both Matthew and Luke make a point of naming the Spirit in this context. Matthew tells us that Mary "was found to be with child from the Holy Spirit" (Matt. 1:18), and the angel assures Joseph that "that which is conceived in her is from the Holy Spirit" (Matt. 1:20). In Luke, Gabriel's annunciation to Mary includes the promise that "the Holy Spirit will come upon you, and the power of the Most High will overshadow you; therefore the child to be born will be called holy—the Son of God" (Luke 1:35). There is a notable rise in the active, effective presence of the Holy Spirit around this event.

The Apostles' Creed picks up on this phenomenon, confessing that Jesus "was conceived by the Holy Spirit." This is striking—the creed selects only ten events from the life of Christ to include in its capsule summary of the Gospels, and one of them is the miraculous conception by the Holy Spirit. The creed helpfully underlines not only the miracle of the incarnation but in particular the special role of the Holy Spirit in the life of Jesus Christ. If we were in any danger of overlooking what Matthew and Luke said briefly near the start of their Gospels, the creed sets it up as the very opening comment about the Son's incarnation. Obviously it has to be chronologically first; conception precedes birth (and his birth from the Virgin Mary is the next line in the creed). But the fact that it could have gone unmentioned rather than being included among the top ten items means that the creed is signaling to us its foundational significance. We really gain from going out of our way to mention the Holy Spirit as the superintendent of the Son taking on our human nature. The entirety of the Son's incarnate work, we might say, is under the shadow of his wing.

Of course we need to bear in mind that the Spirit's special work in the Son's incarnation is not an action that is somehow divided from the Trinity. As Abraham Kuyper (1837–1920) reminds us:

> Like all other outgoing works of God, the preparation of the body of Christ is a divine work common to the three Persons. It is erroneous to say that the Holy Spirit is the Creator of the body of Jesus, or as some have expressed it, "That the Holy Spirit was the Father of Christ, according to His human nature." Such representations must be rejected, since they destroy the confession of the Holy Trinity.[2]

When thinking about the Trinity's inseparable outward operations, we have learned to invoke the prepositional triad, "from the Father, through the Son, in the Holy Spirit." Kuyper does not quite use those words here, but he does explain how all three persons can be seen to be at work in the single action of forming the human nature of Christ: "As the correlated acts of the Father and the Son in Creation and Providence receive animation and perfection through the Holy Spirit, so there is in the Incarnation a peculiar act of the Holy Spirit through which the acts of Father and Son in this mystery receive completion and manifestation."[3]

The word *incarnation*, as we can see, has both a narrower and a broader meaning. Sometimes when we say "incarnation" we mean, narrowly, the action we have just been discussing: the

---

2. Abraham Kuyper, *The Work of the Holy Spirit* (New York: Funk & Wagnalls, 1900), 80.

3. Kuyper, *Work of the Holy Spirit*, 81. We might paraphrase him as saying, "From the Father and Son, in the Holy Spirit." The entire section from pages 79 to 93 is worth consulting for its treatment of the Spirit and the incarnation.

act of taking on human nature, and especially the beginning of that act in Christ's conception by the Holy Spirit and birth from the Virgin Mary. In this sense, we think of the incarnation especially at Christmas. But sometimes we use the word much more broadly, referring to the entire life of Christ, "the days of his flesh" as Hebrews calls it (Heb. 5:7). In this broader sense, Christ's incarnation includes Christmas, Easter, and the ascension into heaven.[4]

When studying the Holy Spirit's work in Christ, we happen to learn the same exact lesson from both the narrower and broader meanings. That is, when we recognize that in the conception of Christ, the Holy Spirit is the immediate agent in whom the Trinitarian action takes place (from the Father, through the Son, but decisively *in* the Spirit), we are glimpsing what is true of the entire earthly ministry of the incarnate one. It all takes place in the power and presence of the Holy Spirit.

The real showpiece for the Spirit's presence in the life of Jesus Christ also comes early in the Gospels. The baptism of Jesus by John the Baptist in the Jordan River is the event that inaugurates the public ministry of Jesus as Messiah. Here he steps forward and begins his work as a teacher, calling disciples and beginning the miraculous ministry that will end in his death and resurrection in Jerusalem. The voice of God the Father sounds out from heaven here, declaring Jesus as his beloved, well-pleasing Son. But just before the voice, there is a visible sign: "When Jesus also had been baptized and was praying, the heavens were opened, and the Holy Spirit descended on him in bodily form, like a dove" (Luke 3:21–22). This is an astonishing

---

4. Indeed, in the broadest sense, the state of incarnation continues even beyond that, since the Son of God will not relinquish his human nature. In a book on Christology, it would be important to emphasize the permanence of the incarnation. But for pneumatology, our point is only that the Spirit's identity is conspicuous when we study the work of Jesus Christ on earth.

event, an epiphany designed to draw our attention to the activity of the entire Trinity in the work of Christ. It is the Son who is of course at the center of it all, but at this singular event, the Father and the Spirit also make themselves known via sound and sight. Here the voice of the Father and a vision of the Holy Spirit are conspicuous. "The primitive Christians used to say to any that doubted of the Trinity, *abi ad Jordanem et videbis*, Go to Jordan and you will see it."[5]

What does it mean that the Spirit "descended on him in bodily form, like a dove"? There is so much left unexplained in the brief story: Did the Spirit land? Where? For how long? And there are also many conclusions that we should definitely avoid drawing from the story. The third person of the Trinity is not a bird, did not become permanently incarnate as a dove, did not take bird nature into union with himself. Nor should we read this as some kind of superhero origin story explaining where Jesus Christ got his powers before he started his adventures, or (worst of all, not just a bad idea but an actual heresy) got promoted from being normal to being the Son of God. And finally, we should certainly not think of this as the story of how Jesus Christ met the Holy Spirit. This was not their first meeting! And perhaps this denial helps us focus on what we should actually affirm about the descent of the dove on Jesus in the Jordan. It displays to us, conspicuously, the connection between the Son and the Holy Spirit. It makes visible that invisible reality that the Son and Spirit arrive on the scene of salvation together, work out the will of the Father together, and all because they eternally exist together in the invincible unity of the one God. The Spirit comes down onto the incarnate Son to show in visible form what the voice of the Father

---

5. Edmund Polhill, *Precious Faith Considered in Its Nature, Working, and Growth* (London: Thomas Cockerill, 1675), 354.

speaks: this is the well-pleasing Son, the beloved one. It is the same message twice, in Father form and in Spirit form. It enshrines the identity of Jesus in his eternal, personal sonship in eternity and in that same sonship, now incarnate and perfectly obedient in history.

The Gospels will not show us the Holy Spirit again in a visible sign; that won't occur until Pentecost. But they proceed on the assumption that, having told us that Jesus was conceived by the Holy Spirit and having shown us that the Spirit descended on his ministry at its inauguration, we should understand that the invisible Spirit is pervasively present and active. They remind us of this truth at a few crucial points. Consider how Luke introduces Jesus's moment of exultation in the Father's will:

> In that same hour he rejoiced in the Holy Spirit and said, "I thank you, Father, Lord of heaven and earth, that you have hidden these things from the wise and understanding and revealed them to little children; yes, Father, for such was your gracious will. All things have been handed over to me by my Father, and no one knows who the Son is except the Father, or who the Father is except the Son and anyone to whom the Son chooses to reveal him." (Luke 10:21-22)

Our attention is focused on Jesus, and his attention is focused on the Father, but the actual rejoicing is taking place "in the Holy Spirit."

Such is the entire life of Christ. Throughout his work, Jesus was led by the Holy Spirit, empowered by the Holy Spirit, and rejoiced in the Holy Spirit. To study the life and work of Jesus in the Gospels is to see the person and work of the Holy Spirit in him. The point of the Gospels is to present the life of Jesus Christ to us, and they do so under the inspiration of the Holy Spirit, who focuses his work on making Christ known in these texts. Perhaps paradoxically, it is in the very act of making Christ known that the Holy Spirit makes himself known as well.

Threefold Office of the Anointed One

Time would fail us if we traced the Son-Spirit connection through each event in Jesus's life. Delving into the Spirit's presence in each of those mysteries of the life of Jesus is a rich and rewarding project that anybody can do with a Bible and a few Trinitarian pointers. We have just looked at the Spirit's work in the beginning of Jesus's life and ministry (conception and baptism), and in a moment we will look at the completion (ascension and seating at the right hand of the Father). For introductory purposes, that will have to suffice. Between these open-and-close parentheses, however, is all that Jesus Christ did for us in the Holy Spirit. To survey it, we can turn our attention from the life of Jesus, considered more biographically, to his work of salvation, considered more theologically.

One helpful way of organizing the elements of the saving work of Jesus is to consider it under three offices, Christ as prophet, priest, and king. These three offices are Old Testament categories, and in the Old Testament they were more or less distinct offices filled by different people. Consider David's command regarding his son Solomon, to "let Zadok the priest and Nathan the prophet . . . anoint him king over Israel (1 Kings 1:34). But when Christ fulfills all three of these roles spiritually, we no longer speak of them as three offices but as a single, threefold office. John Calvin, who was the first to give extended consideration to this threefold office of Christ, introduces it this way: "In order that faith may find a firm basis for salvation in Christ, and thus rest in him, this principle must be laid down: the office enjoined upon Christ by the Father consists of three parts. For he was given to be prophet, king and priest."[6] From here, Calvin dives into an exposition of the ways in which Christ fulfills each of these roles in his one comprehensive ministry. It is a rich study.

But we should pay close attention to the work of the Holy Spirit in the threefold office. Though Calvin may not always mention the Holy Spirit by name when he explains the threefold office, the Spirit is in fact the whole point. What prophet, priest, and king have in common is that they are all set apart by God and anointed to fulfill their tasks. The anointing, symbolized by the ritual application of oil, was a special endowment by the Holy Spirit on prophets, priests, and kings. Each of them was anointed, or christened, or Christ-ed, by the Spirit. And this is the key to Calvin's choice of these three roles as the ones that find their center in Jesus who is the Christ, the uniquely anointed one. As the Christ, he perfectly carries out the purpose of christening. The anointed one has the one anointing.

This has layers of pneumatological meaning for us. First, it leads us to recognize that the Messiah himself would not be who he is without the presence of the Holy Spirit. The Messiah is not the same person as the Holy Spirit, but they go together. The Messiah is the person who is truly and fully and ultimately anointed by the Holy Spirit. They are very close together, as seen by the very meaning of the title. Every time we say, "Jesus Christ," we are rehearsing the fact that Jesus (his name) is the Christ (his title, the Greek word for the Hebrew word *messiah*). Once again, at the very point where we focus as directly as possible on what is special about the work of the Son, we find our best instruction about the work of the Holy Spirit in, with, and under it.

---

6. John Calvin, *Institutes of the Christian Religion*, trans. Ford Lewis Battles, ed. John T. McNeill (Louisville, KY: Westminster John Knox, 1960), 1.15.1.

Second, the presence of the Spirit in Christ means that in every aspect of Christ's work, there is a fullness and comprehensiveness that spills out of the historical accomplishment of salvation and overflows into our present reception of it. The Heidelberg Catechism, which always has a keen eye on the spiritual application of doctrine, asks about Jesus in Question 30, "Why is he called 'Christ,' meaning 'anointed'?" And its answer unfolds in a Spirit-filled threefold office:

> Because he has been ordained by God the Father and has been anointed with the Holy Spirit to be our chief prophet and teacher who perfectly reveals to us the secret counsel and will of God for our deliverance; our only high priest, who has set us free by the one sacrifice of his body, and who continually pleads our cause with the Father; and our eternal king, who governs us by his Word and Spirit, and who guards us and keeps us in the freedom he has won for us.[7]

Without losing its grip on the historical work of Christ during his pre-Easter lifetime, the catechism shifts our attention to the ongoing work of the risen Christ in the Holy Spirit. He perfectly reveals God to us, advocates our cause, and protects us—present tense. The same Christ who acted as prophet, priest, and king in his own lifetime, "in the days of his flesh," now acts from the right hand of the Father in the ongoing power of that threefold office, by the Spirit.

Third, the presence of the Spirit in Christ means that the anointing is not only for himself but also for believers by way of intentional overflowing. Calvin says, "He received anointing on behalf of his whole body that the power of the Spirit might be present in the continuing preaching of the Gospel."[8] The teach-

7. Heidelberg Catechism, Question 30.
8. Calvin, *Institutes*, 1.15.2.

ing of the threefold office has always enabled a deeper understanding of the church as participating in the ministry of Christ. The preaching office continues his ministry as prophet; praise and intercession continue his ministry as priest; and gathering as a community within a responsible church order continues his ministry as king.

Fourth, the presence of the Spirit in Christ lifts our eyes up to the eternal communion that the Son and the Holy Spirit have with each other in the Holy Trinity. The messianic work of the Son in the power of the Spirit is itself a great manifestation of that eternal unity. Irenaeus of Lyons (130–202) did not expound on Christ's threefold office in the Spirit, but he did draw out the implications of Christ's very title containing the messianic mystery of God's triunity. In fact, Irenaeus finds the whole Trinity revealed in this aspect of the Son's work:

> For in the name of Christ is implied, He that anoints, He that is anointed, and the unction itself with which He is anointed. And it is the Father who anoints, but the Son who is anointed by the Spirit, who is the unction, as the Word declares by Isaiah, "The Spirit of the Lord is upon me, because He hath anointed me,"—pointing out both the anointing Father, the anointed Son, and the unction, which is the Spirit.[9]

"Christ" means "anointed" means "Messiah," and "Messiah" is definitely a historical category. But what comes to the fore in that historic, messianic work of the Son is an eternal relation between the anointing Spirit and the anointed Son. "Unction" is a title of the Holy Spirit that is eternally present in God's own being and on that basis takes place in the work of Christ for us and our salvation.

9. Irenaeus, *Against Heresies* 3.18.3.

Ascension and Pentecost

We have seen that the Son and the Holy Spirit live and work in constant relation throughout the course of Christ's earthly ministry. That means that when we reflect on the life of Jesus, there is never a moment when we are dealing with the Son alone to the exclusion of the Holy Spirit. The Son is not the Holy Spirit, but we learn about both of them, and the Father, inseparably. This is true of each moment of Jesus's life and ministry along the way, and it is true of his life as a whole. We can consider the life of Jesus as a completed whole by considering his ascension. He sat down at the right hand of the Father when his work "in the days of his flesh" was fully accomplished. It's no surprise, then, that the Bible has a lot to say about the Son-Spirit relation at exactly this point, at Christ's ascension and heavenly seating.

There is a kind of handoff between the Son and the Holy Spirit at this crucial turning point in salvation history. Jesus had told his disciples before his ascension, "It is to your advantage that I go away, for if I do not go away, the Helper will not come to you. But if I go, I will send him to you" (John 16:7). We need to grasp the full meaning of this Son-Spirit exchange, and in order to do so we should banish a few overly simple, unworthy ideas about what the exchange is. First, the exchange is not just about vacating space to make room for another person. Physics may dictate that no two physical objects can occupy the same space at the same time, but that hardly applies to the Holy Spirit.

Second, this exchange is not a case of one person stepping away so he can transform into another person and then come back. That kind of switch might explain why Clark Kent must go away before Superman can come on the scene, but it has no bearing on Jesus and the Holy Spirit, who are two distinct persons. Treating the Son-Spirit exchange like that would yield

The Holy Spirit and the Son   101

the heresy of modalism. Finally, the exchange is not based on some kind of exclusion or total absence of the Holy Spirit from the earthbound disciples up until this point. As we have already seen, the Holy Spirit has been present and active in the work of Jesus Christ all along; he has never not been there. To tell the whole truth about what happens at the ascension of Christ, we should say that up until now the Spirit has not been absent, but he has not yet been *sent*.

During his ministry, the Gospel of John tells us, Jesus promised that "whoever believes in me, as the Scripture has said, 'Out of his heart will flow rivers of living water'" (John 7:38). The narrator helpfully clarifies, "Now this he said about the Spirit, whom those who believed in him were to receive, for as yet the Spirit had not been given, because Jesus was not yet glorified" (John 7:39). From the perspective of Jesus's work in progress, the Spirit flowing forth from believers had to be promised in the future tense: he is not flowing now, but he will flow then. Most modern translations say that the Spirit "had not been *given*," but the Greek simply says "was not." Translators rightly supply the verb "given" in order to complete the sense. To leave the translation at "the Spirit was not yet" would be misleading because readers would mentally complete the phrase "was not yet in existence," or "was not yet a person" or something equally false (as reading the rest of the Gospel would quickly show). But the narrator's next word of explanation is the key to it all: "because Jesus was not yet glorified."

This is the crucial insight into the Son-Spirit exchange, the insight for which we have been prepared by eliminating wrong interpretations. Until the Son's own special work reaches its completion in his glorification, the Holy Spirit's own special work will not begin. This is because the Son's work is the foundation and presupposition of the Spirit's. When the Son completes his work, goes to the Father, and then sends the Holy Spirit (John 16:7), he is sending the Spirit in a new way made possible by the Son's own completed work. There is a difference between the Holy Spirit's presence among the disciples before and after Christ's ascension, seating, and sending of the Spirit. Jesus told the disciples that the world at large "cannot receive" the Spirit of truth, because the world does not know him. But by contrast, "You know him, for he dwells with you and will be in you" (John 14:17). Before the Spirit was sent, he dwelt with the disciples; afterward he was in them.[10] The difference between the two epochs is neither secret not subtle; it is the incarnation, death, resurrection, and ascension of the Son of God for our salvation. John Chrysostom (347–407) explained this passage by saying that the Spirit was not sent until Christ departed "because the curse not having yet been taken away, sin not yet loosed, but all being yet subject to vengeance, He could not come."[11]

The mission of the Holy Spirit depends on the completion of the mission of the Son. Or to put it in terms of events on a timeline, Christ's ascension comes first, and the outpouring of the Spirit at Pentecost comes after. The Son goes up before the Spirit comes down. The two events are sequential, and yet in a striking way they can also be considered theologically as two sides of the same coin. In both ascension and Pentecost, we see the deep truth of God and humanity in reconciled fellowship. Christ incarnate, exalted to the Father's right hand, is a permanent pledge of our humanity existing in the presence of God.

10. James M. Hamilton Jr., *God's Indwelling Presence: The Holy Spirit in the Old and New Testaments* (Nashville, TN: B&H Academic, 2006). Hamilton establishes this with/in distinction from John's Gospel and considers its implications for how much continuity exists between Old and New Testament reception of salvation.

11. John Chrysostom, Homily 78 on John, in Nicene and Post-Nicene Fathers of the Christian Church, 1st ser., ed. Philip Schaff (Buffalo, NY: Christian Literature Publishing, 1889), 14:288.

And the Holy Spirit living in believers, flowing forth from them, is a profound reality of God indwelling his human temple. Both events accomplish the promise of "God with us" in ways appropriate to the Son and the Holy Spirit.

And taken together, both ascension and Pentecost accomplish the glorification of Jesus Christ. Because the Son and the Spirit are distinct persons who are equal in divinity (recall figure 2.1), it can be tempting to try to treat the Son and the Spirit as parallel to each other in every way and make the mistake of saying that the ascension is the Son's glorification while Pentecost is the Spirit's glorification. But this would be an artificial way of thinking, perhaps overly abstract or mechanical in following out figure 2.1 as a guide. The actual biblical account of ascension and Pentecost is our best guide. In fact, both events move toward the same goal, which is the Son's glorification. This is evident in the book of Acts, where the Spirit's work is constantly focused on empowering disciples to testify about Jesus. Before ascending, Jesus tells the disciples, "You will receive power when the Holy Spirit has come upon you, and you will be my witnesses in Jerusalem and in all Judea and Samaria, and to the end of the earth" (Acts 1:8). Jesus teaches even more explicitly in John's Gospel about that dynamic of the Spirit bearing witness to him:[12]

> I still have many things to say to you, but you cannot bear them now. When the Spirit of truth comes, he will guide you into all the truth, for he will not speak on his own authority, but whatever he hears he will speak, and he will declare

12. Alert readers will notice that throughout this chapter I am blending together Acts (with its narrative presentation of Jesus's ascension and the Spirit's outpouring) with John's Gospel (with Jesus's statements about his glorification, which in part means his being lifted up on the cross and his teaching about how he and the Father send the Spirit). It would also be valuable to trace each of these witnesses along their own lines in more detail, carefully bracketing them from each other to make sure we were hearing each one's discrete witness. I am intentionally reading them together for the sake of brevity.

to you the things that are to come. He will glorify me, for he will take what is mine and declare it to you. All that the Father has is mine; therefore I said that he will take what is mine and declare it to you. (John 16:12–15)

Jesus explains the Son-Spirit interplay here at its most profound level. They are interdependent and unified such that disciples can't have one without the other. The teaching work of Jesus could not be complete without the Spirit's subsequent work; the disciples could not handle the "many things" Jesus had to tell them. The Spirit would guide the disciples into "all the truth" about the Son. Jesus directs us to think of the Holy Spirit not as bringing his own truth about himself, nor as glorifying himself, nor as testifying on his own, in any independent or separable way. What the Holy Spirit declares to us is what belongs to the Son. And, to fill out the Trinitarian context, Jesus emphasizes that what the Spirit declares is what the Son has from the Father. All that the triune God has for us reaches all the way to us because of this Son-Spirit hinge point, where the Spirit perfectly glorifies the Son.

The lesson about the Son and the Holy Spirit at the heart of the ascension-Pentecost story is so important that Scripture repeats it several other ways. Consider the Bible's teaching about the Helper. In John, Jesus promises that when he departs, the disciples will receive a helper, or comforter. The Greek word is *parakletos*, which is so hard to translate perfectly that teachers often just say it in English as Paraclete. The basic idea of the word's roots is somebody who is called alongside to help. But its actual meaning comes from how carefully Jesus uses it the four times it occurs in John's Gospel:

I will ask the Father, and he will give you another Helper, to be with you forever. (John 14:16)

The Helper, the Holy Spirit, whom the Father will send in my name, he will teach you all things and bring to your remembrance all that I have said to you. (John 14:26)

When the Helper comes, whom I will send to you from the Father, the Spirit of truth, who proceeds from the Father, he will bear witness about me. (John 15:26)

It is to your advantage that I go away, for if I do not go away, the Helper will not come to you. But if I go, I will send him to you. (John 16:7)

There is a careful progression here, worthy of contemplation. First, in 14:16, Jesus mentions this Helper enigmatically, not yet identifying him as the Holy Spirit. But the fact that Jesus says this Helper will be given by the Father is important, and so is the fact that he is "another." That one word, *another*, means that Jesus and this coming Helper are fundamentally similar. What Jesus has done, the Helper will do. Ten verses later, in 14:26, Jesus identifies the Helper by the name "Holy Spirit" and identifies the Spirit's message as reminding the disciples of Jesus's words. Third, in 15:26, the Helper will bear witness. He was introduced as "another Helper" but soon becomes simply "the Helper." We do not speak of two helpers, Christ and the Spirit; the title has become entirely assimilated to the Holy Spirit.[13] Jesus's own teaching leads us to turn the corner from the Son to the Spirit, marking both their personal distinction ("another") and their inseparable work ("Helper").

13. The same Greek word is directly applied to Jesus Christ in 1 John 2:1, but because of the different context there, it is usually translated in its more legal sense as "advocate." Furthermore, the Father is the "God of all comfort" in 2 Cor. 1:3. It is a richly and fully Trinitarian word! My point here is that Jesus's use of the word in the Gospel of John, in this exact sequence, makes it central for pneumatology. Because of John 14–16, Christians know that when we talk about "the Helper," we are usually picking out the Holy Spirit.

It is remarkable how much Jesus packs into this title of the Holy Spirit and, in particular, how much he thereby teaches us about the Spirit's relation to himself. There is even more here if we focus on the question of who sends the Holy Spirit. We learn, gradually, that Jesus asks the Father to give the Spirit, that the Father sends him in Jesus's name, that Jesus sends the Spirit from the Father, and that the Spirit proceeds from the Father. In the final reference, Jesus can say straightforwardly, "I will send him to you," not mentioning the Father. All of this is true simultaneously, but it can hardly be put into a brief statement; the Son and the Holy Spirit are connected in so many ways at this salvation-historical hinge where the work of Christ is perfectly completed and the work of the Holy Spirit comes to the fore.

Accomplished for Us, Applied to Us

The Spirit-Son connection is extremely important for understanding salvation. The main reason is that salvation itself is the result of the Father sending forth these two, the Son and the Holy Spirit (Gal. 4:4–7). So these two sent ones not only do the work of saving but, as it were, impress their personal characters into the work they do. The whole field of salvation is structured by the way the Father coordinates the missions of the Son and the Holy Spirit.[14] It is a dynamic that shows up everywhere in soteriology (the doctrine of salvation).

Salvation has a Trinitarian structure or order to it, and understanding that order is crucial for us if we are to value the Holy Spirit properly. Recall the trusty prepositions *from-through-in*: salvation is from the Father, through the Son, and in the Holy Spirit. Though John Owen doesn't always use these prepositions,

---

14. Fred Sanders, *The Deep Things of God: How the Trinity Changes Everything* (Wheaton, IL: Crossway, 2016), chaps. 7, 8. There I use the phrase "economy of salvation" to describe this Son-Spirit structure of God's saving acts.

he traces the exact same dynamic in words we noted earlier, that when the triune God brings about communion with us, "the Father does it by the way of original authority; the Son by the way of communicating from a purchased treasury; the Holy Spirit by the way of immediate efficacy."[15] The movement of God's inseparable work of salvation flows from the Father as its origin, through the Son as the one who accomplishes the work, terminating in the Holy Spirit who applies it to us. We are trying to focus our attention on the Holy Spirit by tracing the Son-Spirit connection, so it is especially worthwhile to say more about the relationship between salvation accomplished in the Son and applied in the Spirit. Herman Bavinck (1854–1921) describes it this way:

> There is room for an order of salvation in a scriptural, Christian, and Reformed sense only on the foundation of the trinitarian confession. In the first place, it follows from this confession that the application of salvation is distinct from its acquisition. The Holy Spirit, as we know, though one in essence with the Father and the Son, is distinct from them as a person. He has his own way of existing, his own manner of working. Although it is true that all the external works of God [*opera Dei ad extra*] are undivided and inseparable, in creation and re-creation one can nevertheless observe an economy that gives us the right to speak of the Father and our creation, the Son and our redemption, the Spirit and our sanctification.[16]

It is when we focus on the Holy Spirit's distinctness that we see how "the application of salvation is distinct from its

15. John Owen, *Communion with the Triune God*, ed. Kelly M. Kapic and Justin Taylor (Wheaton, IL: Crossway, 2007), 104. Owen's whole book is about the nature of this communion, but he defines it briefly on p. 94 as God's "communication of himself unto us, with our return unto him of that which he requires and accepts, flowing from that union which in Jesus Christ we have with him."

16. Herman Bavinck, *Sin and Salvation in Christ*, vol. 3, *Reformed Dogmatics*, ed. John Bolt, trans. John Vriend (Grand Rapids, MI: Baker Academic, 2006), 569–70.

acquisition." To say it as simply as possible, we appropriate the accomplishment of salvation to the Son, and we appropriate the application of salvation to the Holy Spirit. This helps us hear the two-beat dynamic of salvation (accomplished and applied) as an echo of the Son-Spirit relation. Or, as Bavinck says, we build up the order of salvation "on the foundation of the trinitarian confession."

If that sounds worthwhile, it's because it is worthwhile. Recognizing the Holy Spirit's place in redemption draws everything together, from the heights of the Trinity to the breadth of full salvation. John Murray's classic overview of Protestant soteriology, *Redemption Accomplished and Applied*, is a compact example.[17] But there have also been some larger projects that track the two movements in two sequential volumes. John Flavel (1627–1691) devoted one book, *The Fountain of Life*, to salvation accomplished in Christ, and a second book, *The Method of Grace*, to the Holy Spirit. To remove all doubts, the second book's full title is *The Method of Grace in the Holy Spirit's Applying to the Souls of Men the Eternal Redemption Contrived by the Father and Accomplished by the Son*.[18] More recently, Robert Peterson wrote two volumes entitled *Salvation Accomplished by the Son* and *Salvation Applied by the Spirit*,[19] handily making the point about the Son-Spirit relation in his

---

17. John Murray, *Redemption Accomplished and Applied* (1955; repr., Grand Rapids, MI: Eerdmans, 2015).

18. John Flavel, *The Fountain of Life Opened Up, or, A Display of Christ in his Essential and Mediatorial Glory*, vol. 1, *The Whole Works of John Flavel* (London: W. Baynes & Son, 1820). The second book has been published under several different titles, but I have given its most conspicuously pneumatological version, *The Method of Grace in the Holy Spirit's Applying to the Souls of Men the Eternal Redemption Contrived by the Father and Accomplished by the Son* (London: Religious Tract Society, 1875). It has also been printed under the title *The Method of Grace in Bringing Home the Eternal Redemption, Contrived by the Father, and Accomplished by the Son, through the Effectual Application of the Spirit unto God's Elect* (London: Thos. Parkhurst, 1699).

19. Robert A. Peterson, *Salvation Accomplished by the Son: The Work of Christ* (Wheaton, IL: Crosway, 2012); and *Salvation Applied by the Spirit: Union with Christ* (Wheaton, IL: Crossway, 2014).

titles and providing ample room for exploring the fullness of salvation.

But in addition to being helpful for exploring the full scope and structure of salvation, and therefore being a theology teacher's constant guide, the Son-Spirit relation also has immediate spiritual value, in what we might call a more critical mode. To put it negatively, if we make an error in this Son-Spirit structure of salvation, we are in danger of misunderstanding what salvation is altogether. The crucial example to consider is the distinction between justification and sanctification. John Wesley put it this way in his classic sermon "Justification by Faith." Justification is being counted as righteous, but it is not "being made actually just and righteous." Being made actually righteous, says Wesley, "is sanctification; which is, indeed, in some degree the immediate fruit of justification; but, nevertheless, is a distinct gift of God, and of a totally different nature." This is standard, solid, Protestant theology. But Wesley grounds the distinction between justification and sanctification in the Son-Spirit relation: "The one implies, what God does for us through his Son; the other, what he works in us by his Spirit."[20] We need both, of course, and Wesley was famous for insisting that the same Savior who justifies believers will infallibly sanctify believers. Indeed, every justified believer is also regenerate, and regeneration is a kind of "initial sanctification," a real change made within us by the Spirit.[21] But for all his excitement about sanctification, Wesley knew that it had to be kept out of the work of justification.

James Buchanan (1804–1870) made this point as clearly as anybody ever has, in a lecture entitled, "Justification: Its Relation to the Work of the Spirit":

---

20. John Wesley, "Justification by Faith," in *The Standard Sermons* (Toronto: William Briggs, 1881), 45.
21. Sanders, *Wesley on the Christian Life: The Heart Renewed in Love* (Wheaton, IL: Crossway, 2013), 77–79.

> There is, perhaps, no more subtle or plausible error, on the
> subject of Justification, than that which makes it to rest
> on the indwelling presence, and the gracious work, of the
> Holy Spirit in the heart. It is a singularly refined form of
> opposition to the doctrine of Justification by the imputed
> righteousness of Christ, for it merely substitutes the work
> of one divine Person for that of another. . . . Nothing can be
> more unscriptural in itself, or more pernicious to the souls
> of men, than the substitution of the gracious work of the
> Spirit in us, for the vicarious work of Christ for us, as the
> ground of our pardon and acceptance with God.[22]

The difference may sound subtle, but its result in the spiritual
life of the believer is striking. To trust that we are justified
and accepted by God because of what the Son accomplished
is to look away from ourselves to his work outside of us on
our behalf. But to imagine that we are justified because of
God's work in us is to look away from the Son's outside work
and into our own hearts. Even if what we are looking for in
our own hearts is not our own works but the miraculous and
transforming work of the Holy Spirit, we are in deep confu-
sion. We may confuse matters even more by thinking of the
interior work as the indwelling of Christ, as Christ in our
hearts, and thus make it seem even more like we are "trusting
Christ" for justification. But the New Testament meaning of
trusting Christ is clear, and clearly aligned with the Son-Spirit
dynamic. Paul knows that Christ lives in him (Gal. 2:20), but
his "faith in the Son of God" is that the Son loved him (past
tense, pointing away to a decisive event accomplished outside
of Paul) and gave his life for him.

---

22. James Buchanan, *The Doctrine of Justification: An Outline of Its History in the
Church, and of its Exposition from Scripture, with Special Reference to Recent Attacks
on the Theology of the Reformation* (Edinburgh: T&T Clark, 1867), 387–88.

"For these reasons," says Buchanan, "it is of the utmost practical importance, to conceive aright, both of the Mediatorial work of Christ, and of the internal work of His Spirit, in the relation which they bear to each other, under the scheme of Grace and Redemption."[23] Buchanan does not lock the Holy Spirit out of the doctrine of justification altogether, as if postponing his work until the doctrine of sanctification though. No, "the work of the Holy Spirit is as necessary for our Justification as the work of Christ Himself; but it is not necessary for the same reasons, nor is it effectual for the same ends."[24] The Spirit's work is necessary not as the ground of justification, but (no surprise) in a specifically applicatory way. Nobody is justified without the Spirit applying the work of Christ to him; to think such a thing possible would be to lower saving faith to the level of a merely human work (the right ideas, the right feelings, or a strong enough decision) rather than a work of God.[25]

Having seen why it matters so much that we learn to distinguish the work of the Son and the Holy Spirit, we should also come back to reiterate how important it is that these two things, while distinct, are nevertheless inseparable. In 1589 John Calvin exchanged letters with Cardinal Jacopo Sadoleto about the nature of Reformation teaching on salvation. Sadoleto brought the standard Roman Catholic charge against the Protestants.

23. Buchanan, *Doctrine of Justification*, 388.
24. Buchanan, *Doctrine of Justification*, 392.
25. Buchanan's point is a very Protestant one. Other Protestants, of non-Reformed varieties, also argue exactly this way. For an Anglican version that is even more aggressively polemical against Roman Catholic soteriology, see E. A. Litton, who says in his *Introduction to Dogmatic Theology*, "The Romish doctrine confounds the offices of the Second and Third Persons of the Holy Trinity . . . in the functions which each discharges in the dispensations of grace" (Cambridge, UK: James Clarke, 1960), 281. Methodist William Burt Pope warns that much devotional literature is infected with "the thought that the Indwelling Christ is the formal cause of our justification," and that "almost every error on the subject is more or less a variation upon this." William Burt Pope, *A Compendium of Christian Theology* (London: Wesleyan Conference Office, 1877), 2:449, 451.

He alleged that the Reformers, "by attributing everything to faith, leave no room for works." Calvin's reply reaches a climax when he makes this point: the unity of the Christian life includes faith and works, because it is grounded in the unity of the work of Christ and the Holy Spirit, which is grounded in the unity of God the Holy Trinity. Here is how he puts it:

> We deny that good works have any share in justification, but we claim full authority for them in the lives of the righteous. For if he who has obtained justification possesses Christ, and at the same time Christ never is where his Spirit is not, it is obvious that gratuitous righteousness is necessarily connected with regeneration. Therefore, if you would duly understand how inseparable faith and works are, look to Christ, who, as the apostle teaches (1 Cor 1:30), has been given to us for justification and for sanctification. Wherever, therefore, that righteousness of faith which we maintain to be gratuitous is, there too Christ is; and where Christ is, there too is the Spirit of holiness who regenerates the soul to newness of life. On the contrary, where zeal for integrity and holiness is not in force, there neither the Spirit of Christ nor Christ himself are present. Wherever Christ is not, there is no righteousness, and indeed no faith; for faith cannot lay hold of Christ for righteousness without the Spirit of sanctification.[26]

In the following paragraph, Calvin joins up his Christological and pneumatological argument to the love and election of God the Father, making the Trinitarian argument explicit and complete. His point is that the unity of the Trinity's work in salvation entails the unity of justification through faith and Spirit-empowered sanctification. Faith and good works go together

---

26. John Calvin and Jacopo Sadoleto, *A Reformation Debate*, ed. John C. Olin (Grand Rapids, MI: Baker, 1966), 62.

because Christ and the Spirit go together on the mission of the Father.[27]

The Eternal Relation of the Holy Spirit to the Son

Our previous chapter, on the Spirit and the Father, closed with reflections on the eternal relation of the first and third persons of the Trinity. We concluded that the Father sends the Spirit of promise in the fullness of time because, in the depths of the Trinity, the Spirit eternally proceeds from the Father. We should close this chapter similarly, with contemplation on the eternal relation of the Son and the Holy Spirit. As we have just seen, much depends on the relation and distinction of these inseparable two persons in the history of salvation. What is that salvation-historical relationship grounded in? What can we say about the eternal depths of the Holy Spirit's relation to the Son?

To begin with a glance back at figure 2.1 (p. 33), we can say that there is such a thing as an eternal, internal relation of the Son and the Spirit. But the figure indicates only that they are persons in relation; it doesn't give that relation any content. While we are triangulating, we can add that the Son and the Holy Spirit are both related to the Father. The Son comes from the Father like a word and the Spirit like a breath. These are different ways of being from the Father, which helps us understand that the Son and the Holy Spirit are not interchangeable or indistinguishable. We can always tell them apart at least by the distinct ways they come from the Father. That's something! But aside from their respective relations to the same first person, do they also have a relation directly, so to speak, with each other?

27. For commentary on this section of the Calvin-Sadoleto exchange, see Michael Reeves, *Delighting in the Trinity: An Introduction to the Christian Faith* (Downers Grove, IL: InterVarsity Press, 2012), 88–90.

Of course they do, and we can glimpse its character in several ways. Consider first the word-breath imagery the Bible gives us. Irenaeus of Lyons argued, on the basis of these images, that "God is verbal" and also spiritual, that is, breathful; the Father inherently has both word and breath. Drawing on a wide range of scriptural allusions (including Psalm 33:6, "By the word of the LORD the heavens were made, and by the breath of his mouth all their host"), Irenaeus pointed out that word and breath have an inherent relation to each other. "The Spirit demonstrates the Word," and "the Word articulates the Spirit."[28] John of Damascus elaborated on this imagery as he explained the person of the Holy Spirit:

> Moreover, it is necessary that the Word should also have a spirit. For even our own speech is not devoid of breath. Only in our case breath is something other than our own essence. For it is an indrawing and expulsion of air that is inhaled and exhaled for the sustenance of the body. In the event of speaking aloud this becomes the utterance of speech, since in the act it manifests the power of speech. In the case of the divine nature, which is simple and non-composite, . . . it is not correct that the Spirit should be considered something alien that comes into God from outside of him, as with us who are composite beings.[29]

If you take the revealed images literally, you can picture it. When people communicate, what comes from their mouth is both the force of their breath and, via the shaping articulation

---

28. Irenaeus of Lyons, *On the Apostolic Preaching* (Crestwood, NY: St. Vladimir's Seminary Press, 1997), 43.

29. John of Damascus, *On the Orthodox Faith* (Crestwood, NY: St. Vladimir's Seminary Press, 2022), 69. As the translator, Norman Russell, points out, "The word play in Greek is important," since the same word *pneuma* can mean both spirit and breath. The double meaning, already present in the New Testament, may explain why the Greek fathers developed the breath-imagery most consistently.

of their vocal apparatus, a word. If you form a word with your tongue and lips without a breath, no sound comes forth at all (articulation without demonstration). If you force sound from your vocal cords without adding definite shape to it, all that results is noise (demonstration without articulation). In successful self-expression, word articulates breath, and breath demonstrates word. And as a result, the listener knows what the speaker says, and also knows something else—that before he spoke, there was a word in the speaker's mind, and breath in his lungs. This is one way of perceiving the eternal relation of the Holy Spirit and the Son.[30] They come to us on missions that are internally bound together, oriented toward each other, and reciprocally conditioned, because as persons in the eternal divine life, they were already in relation and communion with each other.

Jesus takes up this breath imagery for the Holy Spirit in a surprising way; we might say he makes it his own. After his resurrection, he appears to the disciples, pronouncing peace on them and showing his wounds. Next, "Jesus said to them again, 'Peace be with you. As the Father has sent me, even so I am sending you.' And when he had said this, he breathed on them and said to them, 'Receive the Holy Spirit'" (John 20:21–22). As the risen Jesus commissions the apostles, his own breath is the breath of God. The Holy Spirit comes out from him into the life of the church. Anselm of Canterbury (1033–1109) explains the passage by saying, "The Lord did this so that we understand that the Holy Spirit proceeds from him." He goes on:

> This is as if he were to say: "As you perceive this breath, whereby I indicate to you that, since perceptible things can signify imperceptible things, the Holy Spirit comes out of

---

30. In the analogy, of course, breath and word are separated while they are inside the speaker, only coming together when speech occurs. This is disanalogy, where the analogy stops working. Skillful interpretation of revealed imagery always means learning to take the imagery just literally enough.

the depths of my body and from my person, in like manner know that the Holy Spirit, whom I indicate to you by this breath, comes out of the recesses of my divinity and from my person."[31]

Some Bible interpreters call this event "the Johannine Pentecost" because in a Gospel that doesn't directly report the event of Pentecost (an event still fifty days away), it serves as a kind of origin story for how the Holy Spirit first animated the church after Jesus's resurrection. Anselm wisely interprets the private event in the Gospel of John as symbolically pointing forward to the public event in Acts: Here the breath of Jesus, there a rushing mighty wind. Here a chain of sendings ("As the Father has sent me, even so I am sending you," John 20:21), there a commission ("You will receive power when the Holy Spirit has come upon you, and you will be my witnesses in Jerusalem and in all Judea and Samaria, and to the end of the earth," Acts 1:8). And the main point Anselm makes as he considers Jesus's breathed-out saying, "Receive the Holy Spirit," is that the Spirit comes from the Son here in history because the Spirit comes from the Son in the eternal life of God.

This brings us back to a difficult point. As we saw in the previous chapter, all Christians agree that the Holy Spirit proceeds from the Father. But there has been a long controversy in theological history between an Eastern tradition that wants to stop exactly there, where the Nicene Creed of 381 stopped, and a Western tradition that affirms that the Holy Spirit proceeds from the Father and also from the Son. That phrase, "and also from the Son" (*filioque* in Latin), has even been added to the creed by Western churches. This disagreement has generated

---

31. Anselm of Canterbury, "Procession of the Holy Spirit," in *Anselm of Canterbury: The Major Works*, ed. Brian Davies and G. R. Evans (Oxford, UK: Oxford University Press, 1998), 408.

centuries of strife,[32] and while there is something very important at the theological core of the controversy, that core is also surrounded by a massive entrenchment of bad blood, bad behavior, bad arguments, and bad habits. "There was sin here on both sides," as Petrus van Mastricht said, looking back as a Protestant on the centuries of Roman Catholic and Eastern Orthodox controversy.

Earlier we quoted Augustine himself granting that the Spirit proceeded "principally" from the Father, a position that concedes quite a bit to the Eastern position. And Mastricht hoped that progress might be made by recognizing that the Spirit proceeds from the Father "through the Son," since agreement on this would make the controversy "almost fade into a mere contest over words."[33] Overly optimistic? Probably so. No theologian (not even Petrus van Mastricht!) should expect to dispel this epochal disagreement in a few paragraphs. Nevertheless, among Christians from all sides who can agree that the Spirit proceeds principally from the Father and comes forth from the Father through the Son, there is much common ground. It is possible to acknowledge a real, significant disagreement over the *filioque* while refusing to aggravate it into a source of divisiveness.

There is one more point about the *filioque* clause itself, the phrase interpolated into the 381 creed by later Western interpreters, that has direct relevance for our question about the

---

32. Edward Siecienski, *The Filioque: History of a Doctrinal Controversy* (Oxford, UK: Oxford University Press, 2010); Gregg R. Allison and Andreas J. Köstenberger, *The Holy Spirit* (Nashville, TN: B&H, 2020), 273–95.

33. Petrus van Mastricht, *Theoretico-Practical Theology*, vol. 2, *Faith in the Triune God* (Grand Rapids, MI: Reformation Heritage, 2019), 583. Francis Turretin also shows how the phrase "through the Son" can be affirmed and clearly distinguishes the way in which the phrase would be unacceptable. See *Institutes of Elenctic Theology*, vol. 1 (Phillipsburg, NJ: P&R, 1992), 310. Though Mastricht does not tell us who he is thinking of when he talks about "the Greeks," the "through the Son" solution was championed by no less an Eastern theologian than Maximus the Confessor and continues to be a possible area of agreement.

Spirit's relation to the Son. It is a subtle point but profound. The original text of the creed, pre-*filioque*, said simply, "We believe in the Holy Spirit, who proceeds from the Father." The creed identifies the first person, the one from whom the Holy Spirit proceeds by name, and that name is Father. But in the language of Trinitarianism, "Father" entails "Son." The creed does not say, for example, "the Holy Spirit who proceeds from the Procession Maker," or even, "the Holy Spirit, who, as breath, proceeds from the Breather." It does not cut straight to the Spirit and bypass the presence of the Son. Even in its pristine original phrasing, the creed carefully picks out the Father of the Son as the one from whom the Spirit proceeds. By way of name relationship, the creed itself conceptually enfolds the Son into the origin relationship of the Holy Spirit. Eastern theologians can agree (and have agreed) with this important observation, especially in safe settings where they don't have to suspect that the paraphrase "Father of the Son" is a Trojan horse for sneaking in the *filioque*. It may well be that this was how the *filioque* originally came to seem obvious to Westerners; it's just a hop and a skip from reciting "Father" to thinking "Father of the Son" to saying "Father and the Son." But that last skip is a skip the East can skip. The important theological truth about the Holy Spirit that we glimpse here is universal, ecumenically catholic and orthodox (with both words carefully left uncapitalized). That truth is, the Spirit is never without the Son. The Holy Spirit's Trinitarian identity is bound up with the identity of the Son, and the Son is never excluded from the Holy Spirit's essence, person, way of being, or action.

Wilhelmus à Brakel (1635–1711), in his eminently practical multivolume work *The Christian's Reasonable Service*, avoided excessive theological details and abstractions and did not especially seek to engage in controversy. But in his doctrine of the Holy Spirit, he gave close attention to this question of the Spirit's relation to the Son. À Brakel's way of putting things is often quite friendly toward the Eastern view. He has much to say about the Spirit coming forth as breath; he tends to reserve "procession" as a word unique to the Holy Spirit, talking more about "procession and begetting" than about "two processions." Like many classic Protestant writers, he gives the impression that theological rapprochement with the Eastern churches might be possible for churches outside the regime of Roman Catholicism. Nevertheless, the Spirit-Son connection is vital to the kind of richly doctrinal, practically oriented Protestant theological project in *The Christian's Reasonable Service*, and à Brakel definitely affirmed that the Holy Spirit proceeds from the Father and also from the Son. He takes his stand on Scripture and provides an excellent overview of the three kinds of texts that are decisive:

1. The Bible calls the Holy Spirit the Spirit of the Son or the Spirit of Christ (Gal. 4:6; Rom. 8:9; 1 Pet. 1:11). The intimacy of the "of" here carries weight. We should understand his identification as the Spirit *of* the Son as meaning also that he is the Spirit *from* the Son.

2. The Bible says that the Holy Spirit imparts to believers what he receives from the Son: "He will glorify me, for he will take what is mine and declare it to you. All that the Father has is mine" (John 16:14–15).

3. The Bible teaches that the Son sends the Holy Spirit (John 15:26; 16:7). The mission of the Spirit into the economy of salvation reveals his eternal procession within the life of the Trinity. As à Brakel says, "What is true for His manner of operation is also true for His manner of existence. The

manner of His operation is a necessary consequence of His manner of existence."[34]

The Holy Spirit's relation to the Son, enacted among us for us and our salvation, flows directly from his eternal relation to the Son in the depths of the Trinity.

---

34. Wilhelmus à Brakel, *The Christian's Reasonable Service*, ed. Joel R. Beeke (1700; repr., Grand Rapids, MI: Reformation Heritage, 1992), 173. Here I am offering a summary of à Brakel's arguments, all the way down to repeating his proof texts, because I am in full agreement. I have reordered his three points to match the flow of this chapter though.

The Holy Spirit Himself

We have considered the Holy Spirit in the Trinity, and in relation to the Father and then in relation to the Son. We find ourselves now in the odd position of having already considered the most central and important things about the Spirit before even arriving at this final chapter dedicated directly to him. The truths we have already considered—the oneness of God, the promise of the Father, salvation through the Son—are exactly the truths most emphasized in Scripture. And if we have succeeded in focusing on what Scripture emphasizes, then that means, since Scripture is inspired by the Holy Spirit, that we have already focused on the very things the Holy Spirit most wants us to know about himself. It is good news, and utterly healthy, if the doctrine of the Holy Spirit turns out not to be an appendix at the end, an extraneous lump of bonus material, an elective add-on for the kind of Christians who are into that sort of thing. It is wonderful news that instead, the Holy Spirit turns out to be always already living and active in the main, plain things of God and the gospel.

And yet there is more to say in a chapter on the Spirit himself, partly because of the wealth of biblical and doctrinal riches still to be explored, and partly to correct certain bad habits that afflict our ways of thinking and talking about the Holy Spirit. May the Spirit himself lead us into all truth here as well (John 16:13).

The Holy Spirit Is Not a Curly Haired Young Fellow

A lot of people have had a lot of unhelpful ideas about the Holy Spirit, but for sheer oddness, it is hard to find a stranger case than the portrayal of the third person of the Trinity as a beautiful, young, winged, curly haired boy with a widow's peak. The most influential example of this particular error happened in Bavaria in the eighteenth century. Here is the story. A Franciscan nun named Crescentia (full name: Maria Crescentia Höss of Kaufbeuren, 1682–1744) had a vision in which "the Holy Spirit appeared to her in the guise of a youth clad in a gown and a cloak as white as snow, with bare head and curly hair and with seven flames or fiery tongues hovering around his head."[1] Crescentia's superiors wanted to make this private vision publicly available as an image, so in 1727 they sent for a painter and had Crescentia describe her vision carefully to him. Under close guidance, the painter produced an impressive image that became popular among the nuns and their surrounding community. Copies were made, including not just paintings but engravings and statues. Crescentia was already regionally famous for saintliness and spiritual counsel, which helped these young-man-Holy-Spirit images spread.

1. This quotation is from an eighteenth-century biography of Crescentia. It is quoted by Peter Stoll of the University of Augsburg in his unpublished 2014 paper, "Crescentia Höß of Kaufbeuren and her Vision of the Spirit as a Young Man," p. 2. This excellent forty-two-page illustrated article is the only substantial report on the Crescentia affair available in English, as far as I know. See his faculty website, https://www.uni-augsburg .de/. Stoll draws heavily on Karl Pörnbacher, *Die heilige Crescentia Höß von Kaufbeuren*, 2nd ed. (Lindenberg, Germany: Kunstverlag Josef Fink, 2002).

In their purest form, they are full-body portraits of a standing youth surrounded only by light or clouds. But if you skim through European art for its various paintings of the Trinity (all of which are a little weird in one way or another), you can easily spot "Crescentine Spirits embedded into the context of the Trinity."[2] In these Trinity pictures, the oddity of Crescentia's vision seems even more conspicuous. Jesus's face is easily recognizable, and God the Father is portrayed as a venerable old man, which is bad but understandable—part Danielic Ancient of Days, part pagan Jupiter, part Roman pope. The images of these two persons of the Trinity at least make sense to viewers— even if we instantly feel a little pang of guilt for "recognizing" them! But that Crescentine Holy Spirit is another story. There he sits, smiling benignly, dressed in green, beardlessly teenaged or early twenty-something, with ginger hair and a prematurely receding hairline, sometimes with a dove on his shoulder.[3] We want to ask, who is this guy?

It is exactly the right question. As the image's popularity spread, authorities eventually came from the pope to tell Sister Crescentia and her team that such portrayals were unauthorized, creepy, and confusing. Among other problems, they could lead people to think the Spirit had a body like the Son. Crescentia's reply was, "Is not the Holy Spirit also a person within the Holy Trinity? If so, he surely may be represented in the shape of a person."[4] The pope (Benedict XIV) considered the case and disagreed. He issued a statement explaining that these young-man-Holy-Spirit portraits were unbiblical, unprecedented, misleading, and impious and made the church look silly. Under

---

2. Stoll, "Crescentia," 22.
3. Readers may thank me for not including an example of the images. You're welcome.
4. Stoll, "Crescentia," 17–18. There is a masterful monograph on the wider implications of the Crescentia affair for images of the Trinity, by François Boespflug: *Dieu dans l'art: 'Sollicitudini nostrae' de Benoît XIV (1745) et l'affaire Crescence de Kaufbeuren* (Paris: Cerf, 1984).

such strong condemnation, the images largely (though never totally) faded from use.[5]

Aside from being a quirky and (I hope) interesting art history vignette, the Crescentia case raises some abiding theological questions relevant to our doctrine of the Holy Spirit. The obvious one, "Who's this curly haired fellow with wings?" is in fact quite profound. It comes from our recognition that all the details of the young-man-Spirit portrait are made up from thin air. His height, his age, his coloration, his expression, his level of physical attractiveness, his hairstyle, his posture—all simply arbitrary. Concrete visual details, since they are not from Scripture, had to be fabricated, so they were, more or less at random. And this exposes the most important questions: What was the felt need that drove this image's producers and users? What spiritual itch did the pictures try to scratch? The answer is that people who latched onto these images wanted the Holy Spirit to seem more concretely, personally real. They wanted a mechanism to make him more like a person than he seemed to them. Crescentia's own rhetorical question shows this: "Is not the Holy Spirit also a person within the Holy Trinity? If so . . ." If so, then we ought to be able to focus on him as somebody, as a concrete center of our attention, with details and a haircut and a face and everything.

Wherever there is an impulse to force our ideas about the Holy Spirit to be as clear and distinct as we think they ought to be, there is an implicit criticism of the Bible. Sometimes the biblical portrayal of the Holy Spirit just seems too vague and indirect for our taste. If we were making him known, we would make him known differently, more like the other persons of the Trinity—better than what we've got. The story of Crescentia's

5. Crescentia died with an excellent reputation, and these Spirit images are not generally remembered as a major part of her heritage. The Roman Catholic Church beatified her, and in 2001 John Paul II canonized her officially as a saint.

vision is a parable, even for those of us who would never think of trusting a private revelation or commissioning a painting of it. On the evangelical Protestant side of contemporary Christianity, we can point to an equally arbitrary Spirit character, the young Asian woman named Sarayu who embodies the Holy Spirit in William Paul Young's novel *The Shack*. That fictional character, with freely assigned differences in height, tone, hair, sex, and so on, answers to exactly the same hunger as Crescentia's red-haired Spirit-boy. Young simply worked in a different genre (the novel) and had different personal taste for the Spirit's appearance, for entirely subjective reasons.

While I was writing this book, a former student sent me a script from a church's dramatic presentation of the book of Acts. The script included a role for the Holy Spirit, to be portrayed by an actor who had a monologue in the first person: "Hi, I'm the Holy Spirit; here's what I do in the book of Acts." I am confident that the author of that script wasn't trying to replace the text of Acts with this new, chattier Spirit actor. The goal was obviously to make everything more direct, obvious, and immediate. Some of these errors are probably more lapses in judgment and good taste than actual heresy. But they are all symptoms of spiritual illness. More importantly, they are diagnostically obvious instances of an error nearly all of us are more subtly drawn toward.

As we strive to know the Holy Spirit the way he makes himself known in Scripture, we are constantly tempted to add a few details, to quietly nudge the Spirit in the direction of being more immediately vivid than how we meet him in Scripture. We wish the Holy Spirit were, frankly, more of a character, with more lines of dialogue and a better-defined personality profile. We should be vigilant about this temptation and should theologically repent when we see specific ways we have given in to it. For some of us, abstaining from imaginative Spirit-concretizing may be a serious spiritual struggle, but there is a great blessing on the other side. The real Holy Spirit is better than the one we trick out in imagined details, for many reasons, but fundamentally because he is real and has made himself known exactly as he sovereignly chose to.

A Person Who Behaves Impersonally

Consider, for example, the personhood of the Holy Spirit. The Holy Spirit is not subpersonal or impersonal. He is not reducible to a mere force, power, or influence. He is a person and keeps company with persons. When Christians are baptized into the name of Father, Son, and Holy Spirit, we are not hearing a list of two persons and a force, but three persons. Glancing back at figure 2.1 (p. 33), we can see that having somebodies at two of the vertices with a something at the third would be inappropriate. In Scripture, the Holy Spirit speaks, chooses, acts, can be grieved, and so on. But alongside the Bible's presentation of the Holy Spirit's personhood, it also has a constant tendency to speak of the Spirit in nonpersonal terms. The Spirit is given, is in fact poured out, and flows. He is spoken of as an anointing unction applied to the head and face. He shines forth; he is breathed out. Like a strong wind he carries prophets along. He is a down payment, and seals us like an impression in wax. We might say that there are two types of evidence here, which can be arranged in two columns: column A for personal traits and column B for impersonal.

If this is the case, we need to do justice to all the evidence, acknowledging both columns. Readers who suppress column A (personal traits) demote the Spirit to a force. That is extremely wrong. Readers who suppress column B are less wrong but are at high risk for Crescentia Syndrome. Embarrassed by the idea of the Spirit behaving like wind or water ("That's just poetry!"), they may compensate by overpersonalizing the Spirit. They are also in the silly and self-contradictory position of disagreeing with the Holy Spirit about the best ways of talking about the Holy Spirit. They ought to obey him (personal language) and go with the flow (impersonal language). As we've emphasized, he is a person who often behaves impersonally.

R. A. Torrey (1856–1928) made the inalienable personhood of the Spirit a major emphasis of his preaching and teaching. "A frequent source of error and fanaticism about the work of the Holy Spirit," he warned, "is the attempt to study and understand His work without first of all coming to know Him as a Person."[6] In Torrey's formative years under Dwight Moody, in the decades leading up to the Azusa Street Revival and the birth of Pentecostalism, there was intense renewal of interest in the power of the Holy Spirit. Eager to encourage this movement, Torrey preached revivals on four continents, constantly exhorting people to know and experience the Holy Spirit. He was nevertheless alarmed at the way Christians could hear this exhortation and then treat the Spirit merely instrumentally, as a tool at their disposal. "If we think of the Holy Spirit as so many do as merely a power or influence, our constant thought will be, How can I get more of the Holy Spirit, but if we think of Him in the Biblical way as a Divine Person, our thought will rather be, How can the Holy Spirit have more of me?"[7] Torrey was relentless in pressing home this truth. In part, he was making a theocentric point, that is, a point about how the Holy Spirit, as God, is the sovereign one:

> If we once grasp the thought that the Holy Spirit is a Divine Person of infinite majesty, glory and holiness and power,

6. R. A. Torrey, *The Person and Work of The Holy Spirit as Revealed in the Scriptures and in Personal Experience* (New York: Revell, 1910), 7.

7. Torrey, *Person and Work*, 8.

who in marvelous condescension has come into our hearts to make His abode there and take possession of our lives and make use of them, it will put us in the dust and keep us in the dust. I can think of no thought more humbling or more over-whelming than the thought that a person of Divine majesty and glory dwells in my heart and is ready to use even me.[8]

For Torrey, this shift in perspective changed everything. Along with arguments from Christian experience, he used an argument from what we might call "Trinitarian parallelism." If the Son and the Holy Spirit were both persons sent by the Father, we should recognize the Spirit's personhood as not lagging behind that of the Son:

> Thousands and tens of thousands of men and women can testify to the blessing that has come into their own lives as they have come to know the Holy Spirit, not merely as a gracious influence (emanating, it is true, from God) but as a real Person, just as real as Jesus Christ Himself, an ever-present, loving Friend and mighty Helper, who is not only always by their side but dwells in their heart every day and every hour and who is ready to undertake for them in every emergency of life. Thousands of ministers, Christian workers and Christians in the humblest spheres of life have spoken to me, or written to me, of the complete transforma-tion of their Christian experience that came to them when they grasped the thought (not merely in a theological, but in an experimental way) that the Holy Spirit was a Person and consequently came to know Him.[9]

Torrey proceeds in the confidence that the Holy Spirit is "just as real as Jesus Christ Himself," but he doesn't let his ar-

---

8. Torrey, *Person and Work*, 8–9.
9. Torrey, *Person and Work*, 9.

gument trick him into filling out the Spirit's reality with forced parallels. After making this claim in his opening chapter, he goes on to devote twenty-one chapters to biblical exposition. These chapters reassure us in detail that what he means by "a real Person" is what the Bible means.

We could fill out column A (personal) with a full complement of biblical evidence, but we need to consider the contents of column B (impersonal) as well. In Scripture, the Holy Spirit communicates about himself using elemental emblems: wind, fire, water, oil. This is simply a basic phenomenon of the Bible's pneumatological idiom. As long as we are confident in the personhood of the Spirit, we can fearlessly make use of this impersonal imagery, precisely to help give depth and fullness to our understanding of what kind of person the Spirit is. There is a classic devotional book (from around the same era as Torrey's) that consists of meditations on these *Emblems of the Holy Spirit*. The author, F. E. Marsh (1858–1919), contemplated each of the emblems as a way of knowing the Spirit. Each can be traced in a biblical network of imagery situated in an overall doctrinal framework and applied to spiritual experience. Wind, for example, "illustrates His quickening, powerful, penetrating, prostrating, and purifying work, both in relation to the sinner— dead in sin—and the believer, but more especially to the former. Hence we may say that the wind is an emblem of the active operations of the Spirit."[10] Marsh, drawing on a long Christian tradition of devotional interpretation, finds remarkable depths in emblems like the Spirit as seal: "The Holy Spirit, as the Seal, shadows forth the truth that Christ has accomplished His work as to our acceptance with God; and the Holy Spirit having quickened the sinner, and the sinner having accepted Christ, the Holy Spirit takes up his abode in the believer, and witnesses to

10. F. E. Marsh, *Emblems of the Holy Spirit* (London: John F. Shaw, 1884), 85.

his acceptance in Christ."[11] He then explores "the Sealer, the Sealed, the Seal, and what the seal implies."[12]

What is especially noteworthy in this kind of emblem exposition is how it treats the Holy Spirit as utterly personal. Even in the least promising emblems, such as the Spirit as earnest or down payment, Marsh leads with the question, "Who is the earnest?" and answers that it, he, is the Holy Spirit:

> We beg to differ with those who say that the graces of the Spirit are the Earnest. We say no, but the Spirit Himself; not our feelings, not our experiences, but the abiding presence of the Holy Spirit in us. What we have to do is to recognize and remember that He is in us, and not try to realize His presence.[13]

This way of handling the Bible's language about the Holy Spirit pervades the Christian tradition. Marsh is especially worth consulting only because his entire book does nothing else. But if we searched into commentaries and sermons, we would find the same kind of interpretations scattered evenly across the centuries of church history. Spiritually and theologically healthy interpreters never treat column A and column B as mutually exclusive.

If somebody did want to play the two columns off against each other, we could bring against them the argument that John Pearson (1613–1686) raised in his influential *Exposition of the Creed*. Pearson argued against Socinians, anti-Trinitarians who took the Bible's impersonal Spirit language as the exclusive truth and then interpreted the personal language as figures of

---

11. Marsh, *Emblems*, 35.
12. Marsh, *Emblems*, 35–46. Marsh presents Jesus's baptism in the Jordan as his own sealing on our behalf. Thus *sealer*, *sealed*, and *seal* become a Trinitarian emblem, much as Irenaeus treated *anointer*, *anointing*, and *unction*.
13. Marsh, *Emblems*, 111–12.

speech or anthropomorphisms. Such language, they argued, was not actually personal but merely personification. It belonged in the same category as when Paul described love as being patient and kind (1 Cor. 13:4); he spoke of love as if it were a person, but he meant that a person who had love would be patient and kind. "In the same manner, say they, personal actions are attributed to the Holy Ghost, which is no person, but only the virtue, power, and efficacy of God."[14] In order to refute "the Socinian Prosopopoeia,"[15] Pearson argued that in a case where the Bible speaks frequently and clearly of something as personal and also frequently and clearly as impersonal, the appropriate interpretation was to take its meaning in the highest sense while assimilating the lower sense. There are not very many candidates in Scripture for this kind of treatment.[16] In fact, it is really only the Holy Spirit who stands out like this, and for whom the higher interpretation is necessary and satisfactory. The Holy Spirit is a person about whom the Bible frequently speaks impersonally.

It may be helpful to notice that Scripture also speaks of the Son with impersonal language and imagery—not just the preexistent second person but the incarnate Redeemer. Consider the symbolic language such as *door*, *gate*, *Lamb*, *light*, and so on, which is especially prominent in Jesus's own teaching about himself in John's Gospel. In the same Gospel, Jesus says that he is "the way, and the truth, and the life" (John 14:6). In these cases, no matter how abstract the impersonal terms may get, they are firmly anchored in the personal by being spoken

14. John Pearson, *An Exposition of the Creed* (New York: Appleton, 1842), 465. "Pearson on the Creed," as it has often been called, was originally published in 1659.

15. Pearson, *Creed*, 467, using the Greek word for the figure of speech called "personification."

16. Love, righteousness, the law, the arm of God, and several other terms come to mind, but in none of these cases does Scripture raise them to the level of needing this kind of solution. The figure of Wisdom, especially in Proverbs 8, does call for a higher analysis, but ultimately she is best comprehended under the Bible's witness to the Son.

by Jesus Christ in the flesh, in sentences beginning "I am." But an even more illuminating parallel is the way Paul talks about Jesus's activity in the life of the earliest churches after the ascension. Paul talks about Christ as something that believers put on like a garment (Rom. 13:14), as a subject that they study and learn (Eph. 4:20), as a light that shines on believers (Eph. 5:14), and as a standard by which they are measured (Eph. 4:13). Here is the connection: it is precisely when Paul wants to talk about the way that this divine person enters into the very fabric and structure of the Christian life that he makes use of impersonal language. What the Bible does occasionally with regard to the Son, it does pervasively with the Holy Spirit because of what that Spirit is committed to doing in our lives. Think about this. Impersonal language is an appropriate tool for evoking the deep, personal reality that is manifest to us in Christian experience. No wonder impersonal language comes to the fore when speaking of the Holy Spirit!

The personal Spirit shows himself impersonally when he chooses to. What matters for our doctrine of the Holy Spirit is that we keep a clear understanding of both sides of his reality. As Charles Wesley wrote in a hymn for Pentecost Sunday, "Life Divine in us renew, Thou the Gift and Giver too!"[17] He is both, in person.

All the Names of the Spirit

An easy way to recognize and identify a person is by his or her name. We can and do use the Holy Spirit's name to identify him, but as soon as we do, we run up against another peculiarity of this person who can behave impersonally. He has a name that is not very name-like.

17. Charles Wesley, "Hymn for Whitsunday," *Hymns and Sacred Poems* (London: William Strahan, 1739), 213–15.

Unlike the Father and the Son, whose names inherently show that they are related to each other (as "Father" entails "Son," and "Son" presupposes "Father"), the Holy Spirit's name does not very clearly display relatedness. Instead, his name is complex, made up of an adjective modifying a noun. And when we need to say how he is distinct from the Father and the Son, his name actually gives us mixed signals. After all, the Father is also holy, as is the Son (Mark 1:24; John 17:11), so the adjective doesn't single out the Spirit. Nor does the noun *Spirit* by itself pick him out, since "God is spirit" (John 4:24), and that includes the Father and the Son. But somehow, when that common adjective *holy* stands in front of that common noun *Spirit*, it does identify a particular person. So we have the given name "Holy Spirit," and it obviously occupies its proper place and therefore does its vital work in the formula "the Father, the Son, and the Holy Spirit" (see Matt. 28:19). But it does so by its position and the authority of its being revealed rather than by its own inherent name-like-ness.

Complaining that the name "Holy Spirit" is oddly un-name-like is not the goal here. Once again, we are faced with a choice of whether to wish the Spirit had revealed himself differently (i.e., better) or to accept his name as he has communicated it, and then seek to discern why it is appropriate, even perfect. To see the perfection of the divine name "Holy Spirit," the best move is not to lean in and stare harder at the name itself. Instead, the best move is to look around as widely as possible at the entire sweep of biblical revelation.

Remember that the name "Holy Spirit" is assembled as it links some of the earliest and latest events in the Old Testament. It is from the perspective of exile that Isaiah 63 looks all the way back to the exodus and shows that God "put in the midst of them his Holy Spirit" (Isa. 63:11). That's the most important of the two times the Old Testament contains this name, putting the adjective *Holy* in front of the noun *Spirit* to point out God's personal presence among his people. So we might say that while the name is extremely rare in the Old Testament, it nevertheless embraces the entire testament, from exodus to exile.

The scarcity we notice though is only of the particular combination of words, *Holy Spirit*. That special name is rare, but the person identified by the name is, in fact, mentioned over and over, using other words. In fact, the variety with which the Old Testament names the Spirit is striking. From the first verses of Genesis we hear that "the Spirit of God was hovering over the face of the waters" (Gen. 1:2). In Genesis 6:3 the Lord speaks of "my Spirit." In Exodus, the anointed craftsmen are filled with "the Spirit of God, with ability and intelligence" (Exod. 31:3; cf. Exod. 28:3). The "Spirit of the LORD" intervenes repeatedly in the book of Judges. Entire books of the Old Testament have characteristic ways of speaking of him. In Isaiah's oracular passages, God calls him "my Spirit," while in Ezekiel the narrator describes the action of "the Spirit." In Zechariah 12:10 we have the promise of "a Spirit of grace and pleas for mercy" ("supplications" KJV). As the names proliferate, we do get occasional passages that gather them back together and prove they are all one way of speaking about the same person. In 1 Samuel 10, for example, he is called "Spirit of the LORD" in verse 6 and "Spirit of God" in verse 10, in case there was any doubt. Finally, Isaiah 11:2 describes the sevenfold Spirit who will be with the Messiah: "The Spirit of the LORD shall rest upon him, the Spirit of wisdom and understanding, the Spirit of counsel and might, the Spirit of knowledge and the fear of the LORD."

When we turn to the New Testament, the special name "Holy Spirit" comes forward and dominates the biblical pattern of speaking. After the relative wildness of Old Testament variety, it is a relief when the New Testament elevates this name as the standard. But along with this welcome stability, we also get a handful of new names: "Spirit of the Father," "Spirit of the Son," "Spirit of Christ," "Spirit," "Spirit of promise," "Spirit of adoption," and so on.

What are we to do with all these names? We are to use them, paying due attention to the subtle ways each name brings different aspects of pneumatology to our attention. An intelligent recital of the names and titles of the Holy Spirit from Genesis to Revelation is practically a running narration of the gospel. We can see the Spirit of God enter into covenant as the Spirit of the Lord, hover over the chaos of history as the Spirit of promise, and become present to God's people in a new way as the Spirit of adoption and the Spirit of the Father and the Son. Lancelot Andrewes (1555–1626) admitted that "no person of the Three hath so many, so diverse denominations as He; and they be all to shew the manifold diversity of the gifts He bestowed on us."[18] Once again, we see that what might have seemed like a pneumatological disadvantage (too many names) is in fact a perfection of the divine revelation (so many names!). It is not that God was trying but failing to give us a single, solid name for the Holy Spirit. God has instead competently delivered to us all the blessings of all the many names of the Holy Spirit.

So we use them. But in using all of them, we need to maintain a lively awareness that they all refer to the same person. One of the most important moves we make in putting together a fully biblical pneumatology is simple and subtle: we recognize all of these ways of talking about the Spirit as identifying the same divine person, the one whose clearest identifying name is

18. Lancelot Andrewes, "Of the Sending of the Holy Ghost," in *Ninety-Six Sermons by the Right Honourable and Reverend Father in God, Lancelot Andrewes* (Oxford, UK: John Henry Parker, 1841), 3:206.

the Holy Spirit. This comprehensive ingathering of Spirit terms is such a fundamental move that most Bible readers probably don't even notice that they are doing it. But without this move, the Bible scarcely holds together at all, flying into as many fragments as there are spirits to blow the pages around. Imagine what a disconnected book the Bible would be for readers who refuse to draw this interpretive conclusion. The Spirit of the Father would be one thing, and the Spirit of the Son another thing. And *thing* is the right word, because once you disintegrate these integrated spirit references, your reasons for affirming the Spirit's personhood largely evaporate. The Spirit in Genesis 1 might be "a wind from God,"[19] and the Lord's Spirit might simply be the Lord behaving spiritually. What seemed like distinct personhood gets parceled out to the wind, to the actions of God, and to figures of speech.

It would be a mistake to think that gathering up all these biblical data points under the single heading "Holy Spirit" is a task left for clever systematic theologians to carry out. It is certainly a systematic insight in the sense that all the parts are meaningfully related to each other. But all the data points we have just reviewed (the various names in their various moments of revelation) are gathered up in Scripture itself, in the crucial consummating moment. "The Spirit was not yet given" until the work of Christ was completed. One reason Jesus has so much to say about the Holy Spirit in John 17 is that in that unique chapter, Jesus is speaking in advance from the point of view of having already completed his work. "I am no longer in the world" (John 17:11), he said by way of anticipation, so

---

19. The New Revised Standard Version is one of the few English translations to render *ruach* Elohim this way. In the NRSV's defense, a sensitive reader committed to the full canonical witness about the Holy Spirit might be able to get the thrill of recognizing that this primal, divine wind, about which not much is said yet in Genesis 1, turns out to be somebody significant later on. Most English translations choose not to leave this quite so much up to the reader, identifying the *ruach* here as "the Spirit of God."

that he could deliver the strongest, clearest teaching about the Spirit himself.

H. C. G. Moule (1841–1920) rightly took this passage to be the capstone that holds together the entire pneumatological arch of the Bible. Looking back from this high point of the Upper Room Discourse, disciples can scan the entire coherent sweep of biblical revelation about the Holy Spirit's person and work. The complete revelation of the names brings the Spirit's personhood into sharp focus:

> In this central and decisive passage then we have the Holy Ghost revealed to us in so many words as HIM, not only as It; as the living and conscious Exerciser of true personal will and love, as truly and fully as the First "Paraclete," the Lord Jesus Christ Himself. And now this central passage radiates out its glory upon the whole system and circle of Scripture truth about the Spirit. From Gen. 1:2 to Rev. 22:17 it sheds the warmth of divine personal life into every mention of the blessed Power. With the Paschal Discourse in our heart and mind, we know that it was He, not It, who "brooded" over the primeval deep. He, not It, "strove with man," or "ruled in man" of old. He, not It, was in Joseph in Egypt, and upon Moses in the wilderness of wandering, and upon judges and kings of after-days. He, not It, "spake by the prophets," "moving" those holy men of God. He, not It, drew the plan of the ancient Tabernacle and of the first Temple. He, not It, lifted Ezekiel to his feet in the hour of vision. He, not It, came upon the Virgin, and anointed her Son at Jordan and led Him to the desert of temptation, and gave utterance to the saints at Pentecost, and caught Philip away from the road to Gaza, and guided Paul through Asia Minor to the nearest port for Europe. He, not It, effects the new birth of regenerate man, and is the Breath of his new

life, and the Earnest of his coming glory. By him, not by
It, the believer walks, and mortifies the deeds of the body,
filled not with It, but Him. He, not It, is the Spirit of faith,
by whom it is "given unto us to believe on Christ." He, not
It, speaks to the Churches. He, not It, says from heaven
that they who die in the Lord are blessed, and calls in this
life upon the wandering soul of man to come to the living
water.[20]

On page after page, "he" could be merely "it." But considering
him canonically and holistically, from the fullness of the revelation in its final completeness and its primal integrity, we come
to discern the Holy Spirit himself. The progressive revelation
of the Holy Spirit comes to a high point of clarity and definiteness here because it is based on Christ's finished work and is
taught by Christ himself. There is a famous line from Gregory
of Nazianzus that gestures toward this completion: "The old
covenant made clear proclamation of the Father, a less definite
one of the Son. The new covenant made the Son manifest and
gave a glimpse of the Spirit's Godhead. At the present time, the
Spirit resides amongst us, giving us a clearer manifestation of
himself than before."[21]

To take in all the names of the Holy Spirit, we have reached
out as wide as possible. But we need to take one glance upward
as well. Ultimately, the personhood of the Holy Spirit is not
secured by having such a broad foundation in salvation history.

20. H. C. G. Moule, *Veni Creator: Thoughts on the Person and Work of the Holy
Spirit of Promise* (London: Hodder & Stoughton, 1890), 9–11. Moule provides running
Scripture references in the margin.
21. Gregory of Nazianzus, "Oration 31.26," in *On God and Christ: The Five Theological Orations and Two Letters to Cledonius* (Crestwood, NY: St. Vladimir's Seminary
Press, 2002), 137. I think Gregory is best interpreted as using the label "new covenant"
in this case to indicate the Gospels, and the time when "the Spirit resides amongst us" to
point to the time since Pentecost (which includes the Acts, the Epistles, and the church
ever since. C. S. Lewis makes a similar argument, in apologetic mode, in *Mere Christianity* (New York: Collier, 1960), 143.

Ultimately, the personal identity of the Holy Spirit is something he always already has in the eternal life of God. He brings that identity with him into the economy of salvation. Just a glance upward toward that boundless divine reality is adequate. Our goal is not to get distracted from what the Holy Spirit does in our history but to ground it in his eternal being that transcends our history. Chapter 2 established that Trinitarian background, of course. But it is healthy to call it back into our minds at key points like this: the Spirit is who he is, but not because of what he does among us in the full scope of salvation history. The movement goes the other way; he does what he does among us and is who he is in our history because he has that identity already on high, forever, by nature. Andrew Murray (1828–1917) puts it well: "He has been given to make us partakers of the Divine life and nature, to be in us and to do for us what He is and does in the Father and the Son."[22]

Prayer to the Holy Spirit

"The Holy Spirit is at once the sphere and the atmosphere of prayer," wrote W. H. Griffith Thomas (1861–1924).[23] He made this remark while explaining that while it is possible for Christians to pray *to* the Spirit, *for* the Spirit, and *in* the Spirit, the Bible overwhelmingly focuses on the latter. Prayer in the Holy Spirit, understood in its full Trinitarian context, is the very shape of New Testament devotion. That is why we have already discussed the Spirit "of supplications" in a chapter about the Father and the Spirit. There is a strong and steady directional current to Christian worship, and it flows toward the Father. Our helpful prepositional triad about God's actions is the

22. Andrew Murray, *Spirit of Christ: Thoughts on the Indwelling of the Holy Spirit in the Believer and the Church* (London: James Nisbet, 1888), 325–26.
23. W. H. Griffith Thomas, *The Holy Spirit* (Grand Rapids, MI: Kregel, 1986), 283.

foundation of this. The inseparable works of God are from the Father, through the Son, in the Holy Spirit. Our return to God, based firmly on this, moves back up the triad, "in the Holy Spirit, through the Son, to the Father." This Trinitarian pattern is the "heavenly directory" of Christian prayer,[24] and the Holy Spirit is its executor. We must get this clear in our minds and keep it in our minds as the main thing.

Still, the question arises, can we also pray to the Holy Spirit? More precisely, is it proper for Christians to focus their attention on the distinct person of the Holy Spirit and address prayers to him? The short answer is yes. You can pray to any person who is God, and therefore (check figure 2.1) the Holy Spirit is infinitely qualified.

The long answer is that while it is permissible, there is always something eccentric about directing prayer to the Holy Spirit. *Eccentric* can mean strange, but its root meaning is "off-center." We know that the center of prayer is the Father, toward whom we move through the Son in the Spirit. The prayer that the Holy Spirit empowers and enables is radically concentric, always moving the worshiper into the heart of an encounter with the Father. What is the Holy Spirit's position in this encounter? This is where we want to be sure to think very clearly about what is happening to us in prayer, following the Bible's guidance.

The Son and the Holy Spirit are never excluded from our encounter with God in prayer. To shut them out of it would be, practically speaking, to treat them as means to an end or some kind of optional props just there to get us to the goal. That would mean demoting them to nondivine status, as the way to get to God but not as God. But the one true God is Father, Son,

---

24. John Owen's nickname for Eph. 2:18, the Bible's most luminous statement of the pattern. John Owen, *Communion with the Triune God*, ed. Kelly M. Kapic and Justin Taylor (1657; repr., Wheaton, IL: Crossway, 2007), 420.

and Holy Spirit. We never have to do with God minus the Spirit. We worship, adore, and love the Holy Spirit himself. When we rightly insist on this and worship the whole Trinity, we sometimes make a kind of mental gesture of setting the Trinity off in the distance as the object of our prayer. To do so is a little too abstract. It suggests that Trinitarian prayer is simply prayer toward a goal, which is the Trinity. But Trinitarian prayer is much more of an inside job. Such prayer is, in fact, already taken up into the dynamic of the Trinity, not the arms-length Trinity "over there," as it were, but the whelming Trinity that has brought the believer into a relation to the Father through the Son in the Holy Spirit. Notice the deep importance of the little word *in* for our understanding of prayer and the Holy Spirit. To pray in the Spirit is to pray in the Trinity, concentrically. This is why Andrew Murray says, "Of the offices of the Holy Spirit, the one that leads us most deeply into the understanding of His place in the divine economy of grace, and into the mystery of the holy Trinity, is the work He does as the Spirit of prayer."[25] The depth dimension of the Spirit's presence in prayer is crucial, and it is what we are in danger of missing if we shift from the main, concentric reality of prayer to the merely optional, eccentric devotion.

Another part of the long answer to our question about prayer to the Spirit involves the biblical witness and its traditional interpretation. The fact is that there are no definite prayers addressed to the Holy Spirit in Scripture. What are we to make of this? Only a few highly literalistic Christian traditions have ever taken the Bible's silence here as a conclusive reason not to pray to the Holy Spirit. Most of the major

25. Murray, *Spirit of Christ*, 195. Murray's book, sharply focused on the Holy Spirit, concludes each chapter with a set of prayers. These prayers are all addressed to the Father, precisely because Murray is meditating on the Holy Spirit and is following the Spirit's lead.

Christian churches and denominations have prayers to the Holy
Spirit, especially in the form of song. There are very old Greek
hymns to the Spirit, the Latin hymn "Come, Creator Spirit" by
Rabanus Maurus (ca. 780–856) and Charles Wesley's "Come,
Holy Ghost, Our Hearts Inspire," with its profound final verse
that says to the Spirit:

> God, through himself, we then shall know,
> if thou within us shine;
> and sound, with all thy saints below,
> the depths of love divine.[26]

We also find numerous prayers addressed to the Holy Spirit
in the various liturgies of the churches through the centuries,
especially as subsections of longer prayers that pray in turn to
each of the three persons. The best of them are wonderfully
elaborate and almost always invoke the Father and the Son as
well, directing the worshiper's mind to the fullness of the Trinitarian relations. And these are just the written documents of
Christian devotion; imagine all the unrecorded times and places
that believers have addressed prayers to the Spirit.

In sum, there seems to be a sense on the part of Christians
that the absence of prayers to the Holy Spirit in Scripture establishes a kind of guideline for our prayers. Prayer to the Holy
Spirit is permissible and may even be important for reaffirming
the Holy Spirit's full deity and distinct personality or rehearsing
the Spirit's work. But it should be kept in due proportion. Both
as individuals and as churches, Christians should seek to con-
form their prayer lives to biblical proportions. If you were to
pray mainly to the Holy Spirit, you would not be breaking any
biblical command, but your devotional life would be strikingly

26. John Wesley and Charles Wesley, *Hymns and Sacred Poems* (London: Strahan, 1740), 43.

unbiblical in its proportions. The Holy Spirit himself pushes hard against this eccentricity, both in person and in the book he wrote. H. C. G. Moule summarized the wise position thus:

> While watchfully and reverently seeking to remember the laws of Scripture proportion, and that according to it the believer's relation to the Spirit is not *so much* that of direct adoration as of a reliance which wholly implies it, let us trustfully and thankfully worship Him, and ask blessing of Him, as our spirits shall be moved to such action under His grace.[27]

The full answer to the question, Can I pray to the Holy Spirit? is yes, but mainly you should pray in the Spirit, through the Son, to the Father.[28]

This question about prayer is a perfect microcosm of our whole doctrine of the Holy Spirit. As usual, and for the third time now, what may seem like a liability or complication in pneumatology turns out to be a blessing. Does the Bible speak impersonally of the Spirit? Yes, because he is personally working within us. Is the Holy Spirit's name not very name-like? Yes, because it takes the whole Bible to develop his manifold name. Does the Bible lack prayers to the Holy Spirit? Yes, because all Bible prayers are in the Holy Spirit. In all these ways and more, the Spirit himself calls us to learn who he is *from* him rather than from our random and wayward expectations. "God, through himself, we then shall know."

When we pay close attention to the Holy Spirit in the way he wants us to, we find that he has not only received our worship

27. Moule, *Veni Creator*, 18.
28. I will end this book with a Charles Wesley hymn to the Holy Spirit, an example of the kind of prayer described above, making the Spirit's place in the Trinity apparent. For further comments on prayer to the Holy Spirit, see J. I. Packer, *Keep in Step with the Spirit*, 2nd ed. (Wheaton, IL: Crossway, 2021), 261; and Graham Cole, *He Who Gives Life: The Doctrine of the Holy Spirit* (Wheaton, IL: Crossway, 2007).

but has also sovereignly directed our attention to the Father and the Son. A Christian living and walking *in* the Holy Spirit mainly talks *about* Jesus Christ and mainly talks *to* God the Father.

Neither Listless nor Underemployed

We need to attempt an overall summary of the work of the Holy Spirit, but summary is especially hard here. If you read widely from the best books about the Holy Spirit, you will notice something peculiar in the way Christian theologians talk about the Spirit's work. They make lists. All the best treatments of pneumatology tend to turn, at some point, into a series of things the Holy Spirit does, and the series usually grows long enough that the genre of "list" becomes the obvious way of gathering them all together. We might call the doctrine of the Spirit's work necessarily listful. *Listful* is a real but rarely used word, with two meanings. It means "attentive" (our ears), but it also means making use of lists. At any rate, it's better to be listful than listless (being low on enthusiasm or energy). A listless pneumatology would not have enough to say about the work of the Holy Spirit. But there is much to say. Let us glance at a few examples of listful pneumatology.

John Owen leads out with a maximal claim about the Spirit's work as the consummator: "Take away the dispensation of the Spirit, and His effectual operations in all the intercourse that is between God and man; be ashamed to avow or profess the work attributed unto Him in the gospel, —and Christianity is plucked up by the roots."[29] Owen has a keen instinct for installing the Holy Spirit at the very center of the main things of the gospel. This is indeed the horizon against which we must

---

29. John Owen, *Pneumatologia, or, A Discourse concerning the Holy Spirit*, vol. 2, *Works of John Owen* (London: Richard Baynes, 1826), x.

look for the Spirit's work. Throughout Owen's several books of pneumatology, he generates a number of subordinate lists that heap up the details of this broad claim.

This is the pattern of a healthy doctrine of the Holy Spirit, an expansive claim about the Spirit's indispensable work in the central matters, followed by a glorious recital of several specific items. Basil of Caesarea provides a classic instance:

> Through the Holy Spirit comes our restoration to Paradise, our ascension to the Kingdom of heaven, our adoption as God's sons, our freedom to call God our Father, our becoming partakers of the grace of Christ, being called children of light, sharing in eternal glory, and in a word, our inheritance of the fullness of blessing, both in this world and the world to come.[30]

Basil's list is populated by eschatological realities, from renewed Paradise to our inheritance in the world to come. It leans into the full, final meaning of salvation and takes care to include mentions of the Father and the Son. Over a millennium later, John Wesley (1703–1791), asked to declare his faith, said this about the Holy Spirit:

> I believe the infinite and eternal Spirit of God, equal with the Father and the Son, to be not only perfectly holy in Himself, but the immediate cause of all holiness in us; enlightening our understandings, rectifying our wills and affections, renewing our natures, uniting our persons to Christ, assuring us of the adoption of sons, leading us in our actions; purifying and sanctifying our souls and bodies, to a full and eternal enjoyment of God.[31]

30. Basil of Caesarea, *On the Holy Spirit* (Crestwood, NY: St. Vladimir's Seminary Press, 1980), 59.

31. John Wesley, "Letter to a Roman Catholic," in *The Letters of the Rev. John Wesley*, ed. John Telford (London: Epworth Press, 1931), 3:9.

Wesley's list spans from the eternal inner life of God to the transformation that takes place in us, and then seems to take most of its cues from the various aspects of human nature: understanding, will, affections, nature, person, actions, souls, bodies. But as with Basil's list, we find ourselves more or less guessing at what the unifying categories are and admitting that not everything fits thematically. What counts is not the unstated organizing theme, but the list itself. Doing pneumatology means making such a list.

If you compare these two excellent lists, you notice that they cannot be precisely correlated. They use different images, set forth different categories, and refer to different Scripture passages. It might be tempting to pick a favorite between them or to accuse one (or both) of them of leaving something out. But if you consider them not so much in terms of their content but in terms of what they accomplish, it's easy to see that they are doing the same thing. They are filling out the doctrine of the Spirit's work by moving rapidly through a rich, varied, and powerful series of divine actions. This is standard practice in pneumatology. We could give many more examples, but the result would be a list of lists. The point is not to collect them all, but to notice that the best and most elaborate doctrines of the Holy Spirit take up the subject of his work in list form.[32]

This is a wonderful feature of the doctrine of the Holy Spirit since the items in the list are each so rich and profound, the scriptural sources so inexhaustible, and the resulting lists so voluminous that systematic theology easily falls into the cadence of praise. Counting the Spirit's blessings is not a dry task of bookkeeping but a recital of great things that fill the mind

---

32. An influential work whose length suggests something near comprehensiveness is Abraham Kuyper, *The Work of the Holy Spirit* (New York: Funk & Wagnalls, 1900).

and stir the heart. There should be nothing listless about the doctrine of the Spirit's works.

However, this peculiar characteristic of pneumatology has some dangers to which we should be alert. Lists can be notoriously unstructured, simply itemizing a series of discrete things without attending to their connections with each other. Lists are often not held together by a strong inner logic or necessity; if the inner logic of a subject is obvious, we usually present it in story or outline rather than simply listing its elements. The result can be that we are never sure when we've completed the list. Practically speaking, if somebody asks us to tell them briefly what the Holy Spirit does, we can only give a long series of things rather than stating quickly the one thing he does. Compare pneumatology to Christology in this regard: it is easy to say that the Son saves us by taking on our nature and dying for us. We can say the same thing in more doctrinal language (incarnation and atonement), or we can expand it, but the expansion feels like adding details rather than completing the list. And in Christology, when we expand our statement we generally tell more of the story of Jesus—a narrative series, not just a list.

When it comes to the Holy Spirit though, we tend to just go on naming more and more of his wonderful works. Is there a short formula that serves a definitive function, as in Christology? I do not think there is one that has achieved classic status, either in Scripture itself or in the classic creeds. The two leading theological categories that come closest to being comprehensive are probably (1) the Spirit applies the work of Christ, and (2) the Spirit indwells believers. Those are the two works of the Holy Spirit that I tend to emphasize. They have the advantage of being distinctive, transparently Trinitarian, fairly comprehensive, and open to luxuriant expansion. But it is worth knowing that every theologian who writes on pneumatology, however traditional they are trying to be, ends up making some arbitrary decisions about which categories to elevate from the list up to the level of chapter headings. The choice is more a matter of art than science; from the vast fullness of the Spirit's works, which are the magnetic categories that will draw together salient truths to inform Christian understanding and encourage Christian experience of the Holy Spirit?

One way to see why this matters is to consider what goes wrong if it is neglected. Without a lively sense that we have come to know the Holy Spirit himself, and an ability to recognize him in his works, we are likely to give away his work to others. What does that look like? Sadly, the examples are plentiful. We reassign the Spirit's work and leave him unemployed or underemployed in our theology when we fail to recognize that he is the crucial agent at work there. The problem begins when we think of a task that is vital to our Christian life and understanding and then ask how it is accomplished, overlooking the Spirit's role in it. Theology abhors a vacuum, and if the Holy Spirit is left unacknowledged in a place where he is in fact crucial, other bits of doctrine will rush in to fill the gap. The most likely candidates will be the doctrines or practices that we ourselves happen to cherish the most, or at least are the most excited about at the moment. A helpful way to diagnose this Spirit-forgetfulness is to tune our ears for the Trinity. The cadence we ought to hear is Father, Son, and Holy Spirit. If we hear something else filling in that final spot, it may indicate an underemployed Spirit whose work has been reassigned to others.

The great Dominican theologian Yves Congar (1904–1995) once described recurring problems in his church this way, under the heading of "Substitutes for the Holy Spirit."[33] Though a loyal Roman Catholic, Congar quotes a number of Catholic theologians whose version of the Christian faith was that it came to us from Father, Son, and the pope in Rome. That is, the way they talked and wrote about salvation got right down to the crucial point of where it made contact with our own lives and substituted the church's authority for the Holy Spirit. Other regrettable formulations seemed to Congar "to have replaced the Holy Spirit and let him be overshadowed" by the presence of the Eucharist. Finally, he quotes a Roman Catholic laywoman who testified, "When I began the study of Catholic theology, every place I expected to find an exposition of the doctrine of the Holy Spirit, I found Mary. What Protestants universally attribute to the action of the Holy Spirit was attributed to Mary."[34] The road to recovery is regaining a clear understanding of the Holy Spirit's own indispensable work.[35]

These are hardly our problems on the Protestant side, and especially among evangelicals. When we leave a Spirit-shaped hole in our theology, what rushes in to fill it is sometimes our high view of Scripture. There is a way of talking about salvation that jumps from "the Father sent his Son" all the way to "believe in the authority and truthfulness of the Bible" without mentioning the Holy Spirit along the way. We can, in other words, give the impression that our faith is in the Father, the Son, and the Holy Scriptures. An imbalance like this is hard to correct, precisely because what's wrong with it does not lie in anything it affirms. The Bible really is the authoritative and

33. Yves Congar, *I Believe in the Holy Spirit* (1979; repr., New York: Crossroad, 1997), 1:160–64.

34. Congar, *I Believe*, 163. The quotation is from Elsie Gibson, "Mary and the Protestant Mind," *Review for Religious* 24 (1965): 397.

35. Congar's multivolume work on the Holy Spirit testifies to his own project of strengthening Roman Catholic pneumatology. For some of the same critiques of Roman Catholic pneumatology put in a more polemical light, see B. B. Warfield, "Introductory Note," in Kuyper, *Work of the Holy Spirit*.

trustworthy word of God. What's wrong with this version of the faith is what's missing, or mislocated. The work of the Spirit in bringing us to faith in Christ, and the work of the Spirit in inspiring the Scriptures, is the necessary foundation. Without the work of the Holy Spirit, as John Owen said, we have neither Jesus Christ's death and resurrection applied to us for our salvation nor the Bible in which we learn about Jesus Christ.

An even more subtle replacement of the Holy Spirit—perhaps the most subtle of all—is Jesus. There is a kind of lopsided and exaggerated way of emphasizing Jesus Christ that once again skips over the Holy Spirit in exactly the places where he ought to be emphasized. Imagine a gospel presentation that talked about Jesus dying, rising again, ascending into heaven, and then coming to live in our hearts. Once again, each of the statements is true. But where the Bible turns its attention to the outpouring of the Holy Spirit, this way of talking replaces him with more work of Jesus. The cadence here, quite frustratingly, goes Father, Son, and Son Again. It's almost impossible for theology to be too Christ-centered, but one way to manage it is to steal the work of the Holy Spirit from him and reassign it to Jesus, in direct contradiction of Jesus's own teaching about why he was sending the Spirit from the Father.[36]

Finally, a perennial replacement for the Holy Spirit is high spirits, that is, religious excitement and novelty. Some churches have a bad habit of associating the Holy Spirit so much with heightened human feelings and with remarkable abilities to sing

---

36. While the refrain "Father, Son, and fill in the blank" is a strong indicator of imbalance and Spirit-forgetfulness, it is no more than an indicator. It does not prove imbalance but just alerts us to look around and investigate the overall message. Some spiritually healthy and wisely ordered theological sentences may in fact have solid reasons for naming the first two persons of the Trinity and then something else. Even within the New Testament we have the surprising but orthodox challenge from Paul, "in the presence of God and of Christ Jesus and of the elect angels I charge you" (1 Tim. 5:21). Paul was not guilty of Spirit-forgetfulness, and neither is anybody whose sentences are less Trinitarian in form than we expected.

or preach effectively that the Spirit himself effectively vanishes into the excitement. The association starts innocently enough, with the recognition that the Holy Spirit sometimes moves in great power through anointed speakers and causes real excitement in listeners. But the temptation is to take these transcendent moments in our experience, where we rise ecstatically beyond ourselves in praise and worship, and confuse them with the actual divine transcendence of God the Holy Spirit. Our excited human spirits, especially in gathered worship, lift us up above our normal states. But the Holy Spirit himself is high and lifted up far beyond that. We should not confuse the two transcendences, or we will let the lower one replace the higher one. Anthony Thiselton even hears this temptation sneaking into the modern habit of speaking about spirituality. He notes that the way we use that word, for a domain of human experience, is only possible because the word *spirit* has migrated from the third person of the Trinity to heightened human experiences. The problem of replacement comes up again: we think of the Christian life as something that comes to us from God in Christ through the medium of excitement, spontaneity, intense feeling, thrilling worship, and leaders with great personal charisma. The triad becomes Father, Son, and high spirits.[37]

The Holy Spirit has his own indispensable work, grounded in his eternal identity as one of the Trinity, spanning the history of salvation, extending transformation to every aspect of redeemed human nature, and generating, as it is doing in this sentence, lists of his characteristic mighty acts. The Trinity's inseparable work is always from the Father and through the Son. We should be vigilant to trace that divine work all the way through to its end point in the Spirit himself.

37. This is one of the major themes running through Anthony Thiselton, *A Shorter Guide to the Holy Spirit: Bible, Doctrine, Experience* (Grand Rapids, MI: Eerdmans, 2016).

The Voice You Hear: Scripture

There is one domain of the Spirit's work that deserves special mention here, in conclusion. The Holy Spirit superintends Holy Scripture. Sound doctrine presupposes inspired Scripture, and works on this foundation. But since our special task is to notice the Holy Spirit himself in his works, we ought to turn and reflect specifically on Scripture as an instrument of the third person, as "the sword of the Spirit" (Eph. 6:17).

The Spirit superintends Scripture from both ends, at its origin point and at its reception. When we speak of the Holy Spirit's work in the origin of Scripture, we speak of inspiration. Scripture is the word of God, which the Spirit speaks out in such a way that it is carried along on his breath and has his living breath in it (2 Tim. 3:16). When we speak of the reception of Scripture, we speak of illumination. Readers understand Scripture rightly, and value it appropriately, when the Holy Spirit shines into their understanding and gives life to their powers of spiritual perception. Both inspiration and illumination are the work of the Holy Spirit, and each has its place in theology. Inspiration is best treated under the doctrine of Scripture, and illumination in the teaching about interpretation or hermeneutics. Both happen in a field of divine action, in which communication happens because the Holy Spirit brings it about. The overarching principle is that the Scriptures must be read in the power of the same Spirit by whom they were written. Inspiration and illumination belong to the same continuum of God communicating, and both are works of the same Spirit.

To know the Spirit in Scripture, we should obviously review the statements about him there—how he is named, how he is described, and how he works. We can gather out these passages, perhaps several hundred of them, consider them all together, and build up our doctrine of the Holy Spirit. But those verses about the Holy Spirit are a mere subset of all the verses in Scripture, and not an especially large subset. What we especially need to recognize in order to know the Spirit in Scripture is that all the verses in the Bible are directly superintended by the Holy Spirit. The whole book is his. Think of it this way: There are Bibles which print the words of Jesus in red. But if you tried to make a Bible that printed the words of the Holy Spirit in a special color, you would have to print the whole Bible in that color, a black-letter edition.

Some of the words of Scripture, however, are reported words spoken by the Father or the Son. We read that the Father said, "This is my beloved Son; listen to him" (Mark 9:7), and the Son said, "He who sent me is with me" (John 8:29). The Father and the Son even speak to each other.[38] What we need to notice now is that even these words spoken by the first and second persons are delivered by the power of the third person. The Holy Spirit inspired the writer and illumines the reader who hears the Father saying, "This is my beloved Son." The fact that the Spirit brings about this communication does not take these words out of the mouth of the Father. Rather, it is the Spirit's work that puts them in the Father's mouth to begin with (in the sense of their being inscripturated to reach us). When we first realize just how pervasive the Spirit's work is in the entire phenomenon of Holy Scripture, it can seem a bit overwhelming. That is good. The Bible is the Spirit's domain, and to know God in Scripture is to know God in the Holy Spirit. Once you are immersed in the scriptural field of revelation, you are surrounded by the Spirit. Even the sentences about the Spirit are spoken in the

---

38. Madison Pierce has pointed out that in Hebrews, where the Father and the Son speak to each other, the Holy Spirit does not join their conversation as a third partner. Instead, the Spirit speaks from the Father and the Son to the church, indeed to the "us" who are hearing and reading today. Madison N. Pierce, *Divine Discourse in the Epistle to the Hebrews* (Cambridge, UK: Cambridge University Press, 2020).

Spirit. When the Father says, "I will pour out my Spirit on all flesh" (Joel 2:28), this is spoken in the same Spirit who speaks in the prophets and will be poured out by the Son. The Bible is the Spirit's book, all throughout, and it is always him with whom we have to do.

But putting it this way also helps point out another of those paradoxes about our knowledge of the Spirit. It is (for the final time) the kind of unexpected paradox that can initially be disappointing or seem to be a disadvantage. The paradox is that in this book, the Bible, which is entirely superintended by the Holy Spirit, the Spirit is almost never a speaking character. Though all the words of Scripture are his, very few of them have the form of his own first-person discourse set apart as direct quotation: "Thus says the Spirit," or, "I am the Holy Spirit," or, "I, the Holy Spirit, say this." The exceptions are so few that we can review them briefly. In Acts 10:19–20 the Spirit tells Peter to go and meet with three men he has sent to him. And in Acts 13:2, as the church prayed, "the Holy Spirit said, 'Set apart for me Barnabas and Saul for the work to which I have called them.'"[39] We have now reviewed all the evidence.[40]

What are we to make of the scarcity of direct speech by the Spirit? The best explanation is the one that traces it back to the clearly known character and conduct of the Holy Spirit. Jesus told his disciples what kind of teacher the Holy Spirit would prove to be:

39. Both passages mark important turns in the history Acts is tracing: directing Peter to Cornelius the Gentile, and commissioning Paul and Barnabas to launch out from Antioch. It is striking that the Holy Spirit, who has been driving this movement forward throughout Acts, steps forward in these two cases to authorize more directly the way the mission is expanding.

40. James Elder Cumming (*Through the Eternal Spirit, A Biblical Study on the Holy Ghost* [Chicago: Revell, 1896], 52), suggests a few other possible texts. In the charges that Christ gives to the first three churches in Revelation, he says, "Hear what the Spirit says to the churches," and then gives a message (2:7, 11, 17). It seems to me that the messages following should not be considered direct speech by the Spirit. Instead, they function like the same formula does when it is used in the last four charges with no message following.

When the Spirit of truth comes, he will guide you into all the truth, for he will not speak on his own authority, but whatever he hears he will speak, and he will declare to you the things that are to come. He will glorify me, for he will take what is mine and declare it to you. All that the Father has is mine; therefore I said that he will take what is mine and declare it to you. (John 16:13–15)

The pervasive indirectness of the Spirit's voice in Scripture is the literary expression of his Trinitarian character. He glorifies Christ by setting him forward; Christ glorifies the Father by being the one who speaks the words given to him by the Father (John 14:10). If we were left to our own devices to think of how the Holy Spirit should make himself known textually, we would probably invent something more direct: a speaking Spirit with lines of dialogue in which he explains who he is. It would be a kind of autobiography of the Holy Spirit. What we actually have may frustrate those unexamined expectations, but it is obviously better. The Spirit shows us who he eternally is by mainly telling us about the Father and the Son, and especially by letting us hear the Father speak through the Son. All Scripture is from the Father, through the Son, in the Holy Spirit. Some Scripture makes this obvious even in its expressive form. The result is that when we set out to know the Holy Spirit in Holy Scripture, we actually come to know him in all of Scripture. He is not just in the Spirit-themed verses but in every word, ready to be recognized in the way he has freely chosen to make himself known.

When we come to know the Spirit himself in Scripture, we receive not only knowledge and information, but a personal acquaintance with him. When the Spirit who inspired the Scriptures closes the loop or completes the circuit by illuminating them, we come to a true spiritual apprehension of the doctrinal content of Scripture, but also something more. In describing what that something is, we come to the very edge of what is speakable, because it is a reality that runs deeper than words. To know God in Scripture, through his own word and by his own Holy Spirit, is to receive in our very selves the testimony of the one who speaks in the text. He, the selfsame Spirit, cotestifies in us what he testified in the writing. Robert Candlish (1806–1873) called this confirming testimony of the Spirit his homologation, from the Greek word for testimony (*homologeō*). The indwelling Holy Spirit homologates now what the inspiring Holy Spirit inscribed then:

> He may, as it were, in our presence and to our satisfaction, before whom he is cited as a witness, homologate what he dictated ages ago; and so expressly signify, by some unquestionable demonstration of his power, his actual concurrence now in what was said or written then, as to make it strictly and directly his testimony to us personally; and his testimony brought down to the present hour. Thus, in the word, we have the deposition of the Spirit as first and principal witness in this great cause; we have the precise matter of his testimony. And we have it, not merely as the written report of former evidence, but as evidence emitted anew by him to us now.[41]

The Holy Spirit makes himself known to us in a way that is better than we could have expected or imagined for ourselves. He is the prevenient person, always already at work, never Father-free or Sonless in his being or in his work, closer to us than our own breath, and making known to us in the depths of our selves the deep things of God. We close with Charles

---

41. Robert S. Candlish on 1 John 5:7, in *The First Epistle of John Expounded in a Series of Lectures*, vol. 2 (Edinburgh: Adam & Charles Black, 1870), 203–4.

Wesley's hymn invoking the "divine Interpreter," who alone can "explain the secret mind of God to man":

> SPIRIT of truth, essential God,
> Who didst thy ancient saints inspire,
> Shed in their hearts thy love abroad,
> And touch their hallowed lips with fire;
> Our God from all eternity,
> World without end we worship thee!
>
> Still we believe, almighty Lord,
> Whose presence fills both earth and heaven,
> The meaning of the written word
> Is by thy inspiration given;
> Thou only dost thyself explain
> The secret mind of God to man.
>
> Come, then, divine Interpreter,
> The scriptures to our hearts apply;
> And, taught by thee, we God revere,
> Him in Three Persons magnify;
> In each the Triune God adore,
> Who was, and is for evermore.[42]

---

42. Charles Wesley, in *A Collection of Hymns for the Use of the People Called Methodists*, ed. Franz Hildebrant and Oliver A Beckerlegge, vol. 7, Bicentennial Edition of *The Works of John Wesley* (Nashville, TN: Abingdon, 1989).

Appendix

Rules for Thinking Well about the Holy Spirit

1. When you set out to study the Holy Spirit and find him expertly pointing to the Son or to other theological truths, follow his lead by paying attention to those things. You will end up understanding the Spirit better by obeying him than by resisting his pointing.

2. The doctrine of the Holy Spirit is one of several doctrines of Christian theology, but it is also the doctrinal background of every other doctrine and of all real theological knowledge. Watch for the Holy Spirit in every doctrine.

3. Remember that the Holy Spirit surrounds and empowers Christian life and thinking, which often places him not out in front of our attention but back behind our power of attending.

4. Don't try to be more spiritual than Jesus and the apostles by forcing a reference to the Holy Spirit into every statement. Jesus and Paul often left the Holy Spirit unmentioned even where we would expect them to name him.

5. If somebody is neglecting the Holy Spirit, the first way to correct that tendency is to recognize the Spirit's presence and power in the main, central things of the gospel. Resist the urge to rush off toward a special, unfamiliar zone where the Spirit is supposedly lurking.

6. The Holy Spirit is always already at work before you recognize his activity, and when you recognize him, it's because he is at work enabling you to do so. He is the prevenient person.

7. Remember that if you know the basics of the doctrine of the Trinity, you already have your bearings for the most important facts about the person and work of the Holy Spirit. The doctrine of the Trinity is the natural home of pneumatology.

8. Never think of the Holy Spirit as only a third of God. Always confess that he has the full divine essence.

9. Remember that the Holy Spirit is in God and from God. His being from God is revealed in his mission, but it is based on his eternal procession.

10. From, through, in. The outward works of the Trinity are inseparable but distinct, and everything God does is done from the Father, through the Son, in the Holy Spirit. Rehearsing this formula is a great help to locating the Spirit's work.

11. Just as creation is appropriated to the Father, consummation is appropriated to the Holy Spirit. It belongs to him to bring things to completion, because completion is instructively like his place in the Trinity.

12. The Father's promise to pour out the Spirit on all flesh is a salvation-historical reality so big that it gives structure to the whole Bible.

13. The outpoured Holy Spirit gives believers a gracious ability to pray rightly.

14. The Holy Spirit has a double depth, deep in God and deep in us. As a result of this nearness to us, his peculiar office is to strive with us, groan with us, and be within range of being grieved. All of this is because of his double depth, and not because he is in himself anything less than almighty, immutable, and impassible.

15. The Holy Spirit proceeds principally from the Father, through the Son. He is eternally the Spirit of the Father and also the Spirit of the Son.

16. The Holy Spirit permeated the life of Jesus Christ at every point, but his presence is especially evident in the virginal conception, the baptism in the Jordan River, and the turning point where Christ ascends and the Spirit descends.

17. The Spirit is the anointing that constitutes Jesus as who he is, the Christ (anointed, Messiah). In this anointing, Jesus is prophet, priest, and king.

18. Christ did not send the Holy Spirit until his ascension and seating at the right hand of God, because the Spirit's sending is the result of the completion of the Son's work.

19. The accomplishment of redemption belongs to the Son, while its application belongs to the Holy Spirit. Maintaining these appropriations helps us order our entire doctrine of salvation.

20. We must take our doctrine of the Holy Spirit from Scripture and accept it for what it is and is not. Failure to do this will leave us vulnerable to a desire to make up all sorts of specific details about the Spirit in an effort to make him seem more real to us and to improve on his self-revelation.

21. In biblical revelation, the Holy Spirit is a person who sometimes behaves impersonally. If we maintain both sides of this truth, we can benefit from using the impersonal emblems of the Spirit to know him better personally.

22. While "Holy Spirit" is a special, definitive name for the third person, it takes on this definitive form over the course of Scripture, and he goes by many other names both before and after this special name comes together. This is great.

23. Though it is permissible to pray to the Holy Spirit, we should observe Scripture's proportionality and be glad to pray always in the Holy Spirit, only sometimes to him. When we do pray to him, it is also wise to make explicit connections to the other persons of the Trinity.

24. It is characteristic of the doctrine of the work of the Spirit that it is expressed in lists, wonderfully various lists of numerous things the Holy Spirit does.

25. Be vigilant not to let the work of the Holy Spirit be parceled out to other things and other doctrines, leaving the Spirit underemployed. We are most tempted to replace the Holy Spirit with our other favorite doctrines.

26. The Holy Spirit speaks to us in all of Scripture but very rarely in his own person. Instead, he is the one who brings us the voice of the Father and the Son and the prophets and apostles.

27. The same Holy Spirit who inspired the writing of Scripture illuminates the reader of Scripture, and bears witness with us in a confirming testimony in our own hearts.

Further Reading

Allison, Gregg, and Andreas Köstenberger. *The Holy Spirit*. Theology for the People of God. Nashville, TN: B&H Academic, 2020. Solid, current, and evangelical, this coauthored volume manages to go deep in biblical studies and systematic theology.

Athanasius. *Letters to Serapion*. In *Works on the Spirit: Athanasius the Great and Didymus the Blind*. Translated by Mark DelCogliano, Andrew Radde-Gallwitz, and Lewis Ayres. Crestwood, NY: St. Vladimir's Seminary Press, 2011. Athanasius was famously preoccupied with refuting Arianism and gave most of his attention to the doctrine of the Son. But as soon as he turned his attention directly to the doctrine of the Holy Spirit, he wrote this wonderful exposition of early Christian Trinitarian pneumatology.

Basil the Great. *On the Holy Spirit*. Crestwood, NY: St. Vladimir's Seminary Press, 2001. Perhaps the most satisfying early Christian work on the Spirit, because of its balance of detailed argumentation (close analysis of prepositional phrases) and broad scope (a biblical theology of the Holy Spirit).

Buchanan, James. *The Office and Work of the Holy Spirit*. Edinburgh: John Johnstone, 1842. A great example of how much pneumatology a good teacher can get from analyzing spiritual experience biblically. With case studies mostly drawn from

Acts, Buchanan traces the work of the Spirit in conversion and edification.

Cole, Graham. *He Who Gives Life: The Doctrine of the Holy Spirit*. Foundations of Evangelical Theology. Wheaton, IL: Crossway, 2007. A single-volume treatment of pneumatology that handily folds the key systematic and historical topics into a canonical framework under the headings of Old Testament perspectives and New Testament perspectives.

Cumming, James Elder. *Through the Eternal Spirit: A Biblical Study on the Holy Ghost*. Chicago: Revell, 1896. Cumming begins by listing every reference to the Holy Spirit in Scripture, then making remarks about the styles and groupings of these passages. He goes on to do much more than this, but the book is well worth consulting to see just how far you can get starting from a rigidly inductive point.

Ferguson, Sinclair. *The Holy Spirit*. Contours of Christian Theology. Downers Grove, IL: IVP Academic, 1997. Highly recommended as an unsurpassed biblical theology approach to the doctrine. Ferguson starts at Genesis and ends at Revelation, drawing doctrinal points directly from Scripture and handling all the material with striking freshness.

Kuyper, Abraham. *The Work of the Holy Spirit*. New York: Funk & Wagnalls, 1900. Though some of Kuyper's remarks are dated because they were too specific to his context, most of the 123 short chapters of this book deliver sturdy instruction on a surprisingly wide range of topics in applied pneumatology.

Murray, Andrew. *The Spirit of Christ: Thoughts on the Indwelling of the Holy Spirit in the Believer and the Church*. London: James Nisbet, 1888. Full of insight and littered with arresting turns of phrase, this is a deeply devotional volume that is aimed at bringing about spiritual change in the reader.

Oden, Thomas. *Life in the Spirit*. Vol. 3 of Systematic Theology. New York: HarperCollins, 1994. Oden's goal is to restate the classic, consensual doctrine of the Holy Spirit, which he does by way of quotation and interaction with older sources. Oden handles "the pivot of pneumatology" from *for us* to *in us* especially well.

Stott, John R. W. *Baptism and Fullness: The Work of the Holy Spirit Today.* Downers Grove, IL: InterVarsity Press, 1975. A short, biblically focused discussion of the work of the Spirit that has been especially helpful in guiding non-Pentecostal evangelicals into an informed appreciation of the Spirit's current work.

General Index

"Abba," as human cry spoken by the indwelling Spirit, 80–81, 82
à Brakel, Wilhemus, 118–20
advocate, 105n13
Allison, Gregg, 44n6, 163
"and also from the Son." See filioque
Andrewes, Lancelot, 82n18, 135
anointing, of Messiah, 161
Anselm of Canterbury, 115–16
Apostles' Creed, 52, 91
appropriation, 54–55, 58, 62, 108, 160
Athanasian Creed, 33n1, 37–38
Athanasius, 49, 163
atonement, 71, 73, 75
Augustine, 87, 88, 117
Azusa Street Revival, 127

Basil of Caesarea, 87, 145, 146, 163
Bavinck, Herman, 107–8
Baxter, Richard, 12–13n2
"Be Thou My Vision" (hymn), 4
Benedict XIV, Pope, 123
Bible, as the Spirit's book, 154
biblical theology, on the Holy Spirit, 59
Bickersteth, E. H., 83
Bobrinskoy, Boris, 44n7

breath, 43–44, 87, 114–15
breathing, 11–12, 13–15
Buchanan, James, 7, 109–11, 163

Calvin, John, 22
  on anointing by the Spirit, 97–98
  on justification and sanctification, 111–13
  on threefold office of Christ, 96
Candlish, Robert S., 156
Christian life, includes faith and works, 112
Christology, 147
Chrysostom, John, 102
church, participation in ministry of Christ, 99
Cole, Graham, 143n28, 164
"Come, Creator Spirit" (hymn), 142
"Come, Holy Ghost, Our Hearts Inspire" (hymn), 142
communion, between Son and the Spirit, 99
communion with the triune God, 76, 107
completions, appropriated to the Spirit, 58, 62, 68, 160
Congar, Yves, 148–49
connective knowledge, 8

pneumatology
and biblical theology, 7
and Christian experience, 7
environment for all true theology, 6
paradoxical character of, 8
part of Trinitarianism, 33, 34, 46
Pohle, Joseph, 55n18
Polhill, Edward, 14
Pope, William Burt, 6, 89–90, 111n25
prayer
in the Spirit, 18, 77–78, 142–44, 162
through the Son, 143–44
to the Father, 143–44
Trinitarian pattern of, 140
Preuss, Arthur, 55n18
procession
different from generation, 86–87
unique to the Holy Spirit, 119
processions, doctrine of, 45–46, 53, 119
promise and fulfillment, 30
prophets, promise of the Spirit, 62–64
Protestant scholasticism, 59
pulmonology analogy, 5–6

reconciliation, 75
Reeves, Michael, 113n27
reflective knowledge, 8
regeneration, 109
religious experience, 150–51
right reading, 25
Rollock, Robert, 40–41
Roman Catholic pneumatology, 149n35
Russell, Norman, 114n29

Sadoleto, Jacobo, 111
salvation
from the Father, through the Son, in the Spirit, 73, 106
Trinitarian structure of, 106
sanctification, and justification, 109–12
Scripture, and work of the Spirit, 149
seal of the Spirit, 67
"seven Spirits" of Revelation, 25n12
sin, as obstacle of indwelling of God, 71, 73
Socinianism, 130–31
Son
accomplishment of salvation, 71–73, 74, 108
eternally begotten from the Father, 44
incarnation of, 43, 71–73
mission of, 53, 102, 115
purchased treasury of, 77
Son-Spirit relation, 100–106, 107, 108–9
Spirit-forgetfulness, 150n36
Spirit of God, 134–35
"Spirit of Truth, Essential God" (hymn), 157
spirituality, as heightened human experiences, 151
Stott, John R. W., 29–30, 165
Swain, Scott, 44n6
systematic theology, 9

temple, 69
theology, spiritual character of, 6
Thiselton, Anthony, 151
Thomas Aquinas, 22
Thomas, W. H. Griffith, 139
Torrey, R. A., 127–28
Treier, Daniel J., 67n1
Trinitarian parallelism, 128

Scripture Index

Short Studies in Systematic Theology

For more information, visit **crossway.org**.